NEEDLES OUT!

NEEDLES OUT!

Nichole Vogelsinger

Published in 2024 by
Lucky Spool Media, LLC
www.luckyspool.com
info@luckyspool.com

Text © Nichole Vogelsinger
Editor Bruce Darlaston
Creative Director Megan McElroy
Designer Mark Robertson, DEPTHM
Illustrations Nichole Vogelsinger
Color Illustrations, pages 151 and 205, Amelia Pease
Styling El Robertson, DEPTHM
Photography Mark Robertson, DEPTHM

9 8 7 6 5 4 3 2 1

First Edition
Printed in China

Library of Congress Cataloging-in-Publication
Data available upon request

ISBN 978-1-940655-52-9

LSID0061

CONTENTS

INTRODUCTION

Several years ago, I had the opportunity to visit the Christian Dior exhibit at the Denver Art Museum. To say that I was absolutely floored by the beauty and intricacy of the designs I saw, would have been an understatement. If you know me at all, you'd know that I'm most likely to be puttering around in my Birkenstocks and worn denim and not wearing or even drooling over high fashion designs. But there was something about this exhibit that completely stopped me in my tracks and beckoned me into this world. Studying the embroidery samples that were heavy with sequins and beads, something that I already loved and incorporated into my own embroidery, I knew I wanted to do more. More sequins. More beads. More textures and materials. Just more.

I've dabbled in making clothes, but it's not my true love. In fact, I find it stressful. Somehow, the love that my mom had for smocking handmade dresses and creating quilts with intricate designs, did not find its way into my hands or heart! But if I could find a way to incorporate more of the things from these high fashion garments that I fell in love with and add them to my work, I knew that's what I needed to do.

From that point on, my embroidery pieces became noticeably heavier with more beads, more embroidery, more sequins. I searched out threads that were unique and could add varied textures to my projects. I experimented with fabrics beyond quilting cotton: silk, wool and tulle. They were also filled with something that could not be seen: more time. Rather than being able to complete several projects in a month, it could now take me a month or more to complete just one project. And let's not get started on how much extra time it takes when you are someone who jumps from project to project to project!

When I began pairing fabrics I loved, along with embroidery back in 2012, my focus was on the fabrics. Were there cute elements, little woodland creatures, that I could highlight? Did I like the color palette? Were there geometric designs that I could cut out and layer with other shapes? The embroidery that I did was always there, but the fabric combinations were the focus. The fun of playing with fabric and fussy cutting came through in my early projects. Now, 10 years later, my designs have become much more embroidery focused. The fabric is still the highlight of what I work with, but it makes its way into the background as the embroidery stitches, beads, sequins, wool fiber, thread and paint, all take their place in the spotlight.

Why Boho Embroidery? I coined the term "boho embroidery" back when I began sharing my fabric collage and embroidery techniques on Instagram. I felt that it encompassed what I loved most about crafting: the free-spirited approach to a project. There are no rules that must be followed. Most of my projects don't begin with a clear end point but rather they take shape as I work on them. I find that working this way doesn't tie me down to an exact process, but lets my creativity ebb and flow. I have found it a relaxing way to create.

I've never been someone who enjoys baking and I feel that it's for the same reason Boho Embroidery appeals to me so much. Following directions and exact measurements is not how I work best. I end up reading and re-reading and most likely reading a recipe again and again, and I still make mistakes! Knowing that it is not a strength of mine probably doesn't help me relax when I bake! And so, I do not want crafting and embroidery to ever feel that way.

Knowing the basics of each technique is what is important. And so that will be the focus of any directions that I'll talk you through. Throughout this book, I will teach you techniques that work for each of the mediums that encompass boho embroidery: appliqué, beading, stumpwork, fabric painting and needle felting. I will show you what works for me and what goes into using these mediums effectively. However, as you work through your own projects using these techniques, you may discover something that works better for you. And that's great! I fully encourage you to wander from my text and create something that is uniquely you! I do not include pages of exact measurements that you need to follow closely or patterns that must be cut out exactly (let's leave that to the quilters and seamstresses and tailors of the world!). The few patterns that are included in this book are merely guides. From those, you can create projects resembling the ones that I have done. Or you can use them as practice pieces to experiment with before creating your own signature look!

And so, throughout this book, I will take you down the rabbit hole into my love of embellishments, fiber, mixed-media and textiles. If you already enjoy sitting down with fabric, a needle and some thread, then I hope this will encourage you to do more! Add an element you haven't tried before. Pull out your acrylic paints and brushes and dabble in adding some more color. There are no right or wrong ideas. Experiment and create and enjoy the process! And most of all, relax!

NEEDLES DOWN!

Stitching is a relaxing and meditative craft, the sort of craft where your mind is allowed to wander as you bring your needle and thread up and down through the fabric.

When I'm not listening to music or podcasts, my mind can wander a lot while I stitch. This isn't usually a problem, unless I am stitching to meet a deadline and I cannot allow myself to be distracted! So, when I do have the time, I let myself think and then I will spend time googling all of the things that I wondered about!

All through this book, I will encourage you to put your needles down as I share with you random bits of information that I found interesting, whether or not these tidbits relate to embroidery!

CHAPTER ONE

Exploring Embroidery

Embroidery Supplies • Embroidery Hoops

If you are new to exploring embroidery hoops, you will find that there are wood and plastic ones. If you are looking for an easily accessible embroidery hoop at your local craft store, your options are typically limited to round bamboo wooden hoops and an array of round plastic-colored hoops. If you shop online, you will find there are options in the type of wood hoop offered, the shape of the hoop and of course the size. If you shop at thrift stores, you can find a mix of old and new, wood and plastic and sometimes even metal.

Every crafter that you talk to will most likely prefer a different type of hoop. I prefer wood hoops which I often find at thrift or antique stores. If I see them, I buy them! The wood they used on vintage hoops is generally sturdier than we find on brand new hoops. Old ones will not splinter as easily and they usually have a golden glow to the wood. They will always be my first choice.

It is fun to play around with unexpected shapes in your projects, and you'll notice that throughout this book, I have used both square and triangular hoops. After years of using round hoops, I have found these unexpected shapes have become a favorite embroidery accessory! You can find them in the places I have named in the resources section of this book. (Page 202)

It might take a few projects for you to decide which is your favorite hoop. And you may decide to just embrace the variety. The selection of hoops available to contemporary makers is just so diverse!

NEEDLES DOWN!

Grab an embroidery slate and get those needles out!

What is your first thought when you hear that something is made of slate? Do you think of building materials? Maybe a slate roof or slate patio? Is it a slate chalkboard, much like the one that Anne Shirley shattered over Gilbert Blythe's head?

If you are like me, you might have heard the term "embroidery slate" and thought of those items. Would you have guessed there is no slate at all involved in the making of an embroidery slate?

Let me clear up the confusion!

Early embroidery hoops were known as embroidery slates and they weren't hoops as much as they were square frames. Unfortunately, we do not have books on embroidery that can be checked out of the library to show us techniques from those early times. What we do have is artwork and clever deciphering!

One of the first depictions of embroidery slates dates back to a piece of artwork from the 14th century where Mary is shown sewing at an embroidery slate with young Jesus by her side. We see her seated at a large rectangular frame, with her fabric tightly secured to it. There is no circular embroidery hoop in sight! Later, but also in the 14th century, the term "embroidery slate" is used in a book on painting.

Hundreds of years pass by and we can see embroiderers depicted in artwork, usually stitching with the same sort of large wooden frame, fabric tautly attached to all sides. In the 18th century, an encyclopedia of sorts was published on embroidery techniques and in that, there are directions on how to secure your fabric in a frame for embroidery.

Embroidery slates exist to this day and, while not available in your local craft store, they are desired for their ability to keep perfect tension in your fabric. If you've ever used a flimsy plastic hoop, and struggled to keep your fabric tight in the hoop while stitching, you can understand the importance of fabric tension! Using a fabric slate takes more time and patience than using an embroidery hoop. Fabric is not simply placed in the frame but instead you need to "dress the frame" with your fabric, carefully preparing the fabric and attaching it to the frame.

Chances are, if you are a casual embroiderer, you will not need to procure or use a slate frame. However, if you plan on elevating your embroidery techniques to include goldwork, lacework or silk embroidery, you may find that a slate frame is the only kind you will want to use.

Embroidery Supplies • Needles

Needles are to an embroiderer what pens are to a writer. Everyone has a different go-to pen, and we can become quite possessive over our favorites. (Or is that just me?!) The same goes for needles.

If you use a needle and thread on a regular basis, you probably already have a favorite needle. But, if this is your first time gathering embroidery supplies, begin by purchasing a variety pack of needles. This will allow you to try several lengths and thicknesses, until you find a good fit.

My favorite needle is a milliners needle. They are sometimes called straw needles and you'll notice that they do not have a graduated shaft. The needle will have the same thickness from end-to-end. They work really well for embroidery and can also be used for beading.

For certain stitches, I keep several tapestry needles handy as well. Some have larger eyes which I use for thicker thread. A tapestry needle does not have a sharp tip. For stitches like the Woven Filling Stitch, this is important, because it allows you to weave threads without piercing them with the end of the needle.

Embroidery Supplies • Scissors

Embroidery scissors are very personal and so the only recommendation that I have for you, other than always having a pair of embroidery scissors handy, is to buy a pair of the Fiskars® Easy-Action™ Micro-tip Scissors for yourself. These scissors will save your hands when you are doing lots of fussy cutting! The Micro-Tip on the scissors allows you to make the many tiny cuts in your fabric which are essential for fabric appliqué, fussy cutting and collage.

Weeks Dye Works
Specializing in Hand Over Dyed Fibers
Petite Rays
Cross Stitch
Very Velvet
Anchor

Embroidery Threads

I have so much love for thread, and I hope that as you begin to embroider, you will feel the same way! Threads are the primary medium for an embroidery artist, so it is helpful to have a variety to work with and to experiment with in your work.

Stranded Threads

Stranded threads are those that can be separated into anywhere from one to six strands. These threads are generally the most affordable and a great place to start building your collection. They come in a large variety of colors. Being able to divide the strands is especially helpful when you want to stitch with multiple thicknesses. When you are embroidering small details, you may only want one or two strands, whereas when you want a stitch to stand out, you will want all six. My favorites are spools of Anchor® stranded cotton and Weeks Dye Works™ hand-dyed skeins.

Perle *(or Pearl)* Cotton

Perle cotton is not divisible, which means you can use it directly off of the skein or spool. It has a lovely twist to the fibers and can be found both in several weights and in an amazing array of colors. Perle (pearl) cotton comes in four weights: size 3 is the thickest, size 5 is a medium weight, size 8 is a standard weight and size 12 is the thinnest.

My favorites are made by Wonderfil Specialty Threads and Weeks Dye Works. Wonderfil® Specialty Threads makes Eleganza perle cotton. It comes in both balls and spools. The spools are made in collaboration with Sue Spargo. This thread layers beautifully and the twist in the thread adds a subtle texture to your embroidery. Weeks Dye Works carries the thinnest size of perle cotton: size 12. Sizes 3, 5 and 8 come as skeins of thread, while their size 12, which is excellent for beading, comes on a spool.

Beading Threads

Speaking of beading threads, all of the above-mentioned products can be used for incorporating beads into your embroidery. If I am simply looking to add beads without the stitches being noticeable, I use spools of Fruitti thread made by Wonderfil Specialty Threads. This thread comes in 41 variegated colors and is my favorite when I am adding beads to my work.

Textural Threads

Tapestry yarn can be used for embroidery as well as for needlepoint work. It is a thicker thread and so you may need a needle with a larger eye to use these threads. DMC® makes both a tapestry wool and my favorite, a matte cotton thread called Retors Mat. Both come in a large variety of several hundred colors. Anchor Crafts also makes a lovely tapestry wool called Tapisserie Wool, which comes in 475 shades. Talk about color choice!

The Thread Gatherer specializes in hand dyed fibers. You are sure to find an interesting fiber to stitch with from this shop! From silk threads to sea grass to linen, every thread I use, I love! My favorites are the Silk n' Colors, which can be divided up into 1-12 strands, the Shepherd's Silk™ and the Sheep's Silk™. Both these are so soft to stitch with, while their Aurora, adds a little bit of sparkle to your stitches.

Rainbow Gallery Threads carries 50 varieties of fibers to stitch with. As these are packaged on small cardboard spools, it is easy to keep a selection of their threads in your stash to experiment with. A fun variety of textures such as velvet, leather, wool, and silk can be found, and you will notice several of these in my stitch samplers.

Koigu Premium Merino (KPM) needlepoint yarn is 100% merino wool and is an excellent choice for adding texture to your embroidery. It is a thicker thread, but is easy to stitch with.

Beads

Just when you thought I couldn't have any more love to give embroidery supplies, along come beads! Beads are my very favorite way to explore texture in embroidery. Beads, along with sequins, add a sparkle and dimension to your stitching and make even the simplest stitches shine.

You will notice in the samplers that there are several stitches that work well with beads. I typically use seed beads in sizes 8 (which is a standard bead size and is easy to find) and 6 (slightly larger and more noticeable on your work). There are even larger sizes, such as a size 32, which you can see in action on the Chain Stitch sampler.

I use John Bead Czech seed beads for almost all of my embroidery. These are easy to find at your local craft store and they come in a wide variety of colors. If you aren't sure where to start, I suggest buying a tube of size 8, a tube of size 6, and a different shape, like a bugle bead. You do not need a lot to get started and this will allow you to have a variety to work with as you get going. You may love adding beads so much that you will soon be buying all the colors and all the sizes and all the shapes!

So, now that you have all of your embroidery supplies handy, let's get into the embroidery stitches!

Embroidery Stitches

You will notice that all of the projects throughout this book are botanically focused. It is no secret that flowers and leaves are the focus of my embroidery, and something that I really love stitching.

I am sharing with you the embroidery stitches that I most use in botanical embroidery, though they can all be applied to your personal tastes. There are many stitches here that I come back to using over and over again. I have broken them up into three categories: line stitches (for plant stems), fill stitches (for leaves and flowers) and isolated stitches (for small details). I will also give you suggestions for using beads and sequins with your embroidery stitches.

If you are new to embroidery, I suggest you choose a few stitches to begin with. Learn them well by repeatedly using them. Create a sampler similar to those you will see in the following pages. Make them your go-to stitches. From there, add in new stitches occasionally. The goal is to become comfortable with a needle and thread and feel like you can relax while stitching, rather than being on edge because you do not know how to do a particular stitch.

Along with directions on how to stitch each of these embroidery stitches, I created a list of each of the threads that I used, along with any beads and sequins, for the stitch samplers. If you have always wanted to try a particular thread, but you weren't sure what it would look like stitched up, now you will know! It also gives you a good excuse to try out a thread that you might not have used before. And don't we all need a good excuse to buy more thread?!

All of the small stitch samplers have been created using the Chalk and Charcoal® line of fabrics, designed by Jennifer Sampou for Robert Kaufman.

I suggest having a practice hoop nearby while you are stitching. Having a practice hoop takes away any worries that you are going to mess up on your project!

Practice the stitches over and over until you know you will be comfortable working with them on your main project.

Use your practice hoop like you would use a piece of scrap paper.

Have it handy when you need to jot down a stitch!

And remember, if you stitch something the wrong way, simply pull out your threads and start over again.

It's that easy! Again, relax and enjoy this process.

Here, I have created a pattern for an 18-stitch botanical sampler (Page 208) which contains every stitch from this book. Embroidering this sampler will allow you to practice each of the stitches outlined in the following pages, while creating a beautiful piece of embroidery at the same time.

NEEDLES DOWN!

Les Petites Mains or "The Little Hands"

"The little hands" doesn't sound like the job description of an especially prestigious position. You wouldn't guess that someone with this title would need to have at least ten years of study under their belt to work at one of the elite Haute Couture fashion houses, would you?

To be a Haute Couture label, one of the requirements is that the house has an atelier, (a studio) in Paris that employs at least 15 people and that it presents at least two shows a year. The people in the atelier work closely with private clients as well as creating fashions that will be showcased during the runway shows.

The runway shows have a theme and all of the garments created will somehow relate to that theme.

Once the creative director has determined the theme of the show and the garments, the little hands begin working. Every garment showcased on the runway will be made by hand and can take as many as 700 hours to create. From hand embroidering tiny beads and sequins, to adding pieces of lace, to hand-dyeing textiles to achieve the perfect color, "les petites mains" experts can and will do it all.

Embroidery Line Stitches

Backstitch

The Backstitch might seem like the simplest of stitches, and it really is. But with this humble stitch, you can add so much to your embroidery. When you are beginning to work with beads and sequins, make this one of your go-to stitches!

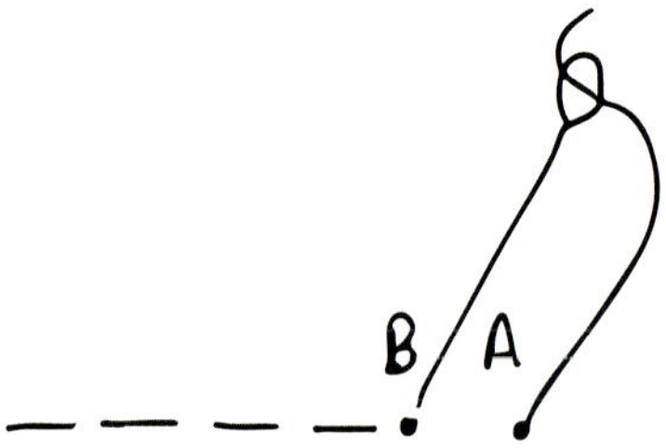

In this sampler you can see that I have added an array of beads and sequins. When adding a bead or sequin to the backstitch, bring your needle up through the fabric, place the bead or sequin on the needle and slide it to the thread. Then take your needle back down through the fabric to complete the stitch. You can adjust the bead or sequin position as needed, to make it lay on the fabric how you want it to.

Bring the needle up at A and down at B. Continue until you have finished your line.

Threads used in this sampler (from the outside edge to the inside):

Koigu KPPPM needlepoint yarn with size 6 beads
Koigu KPPPM needlepoint yarn with size 8 beads
DMC Cotton Retors Mat size 4
Wonderfil Specialty Threads, Perle cotton size 8 with sequins
DMC Tapestry Wool
Wonderfil Specialty Threads Dazzle
Rainbow Gallery, Splendor 12-ply silk
Rainbow Gallery, Rainbow Tweed
Wonderfil Specialty Threads / Sue Spargo, Eleganza perle cotton size 3
Rainbow Gallery, Very Velvet with size 2 seed beads
Silk Ribbon
DMC Cotton Retors Mat size 4

Stem Stitch

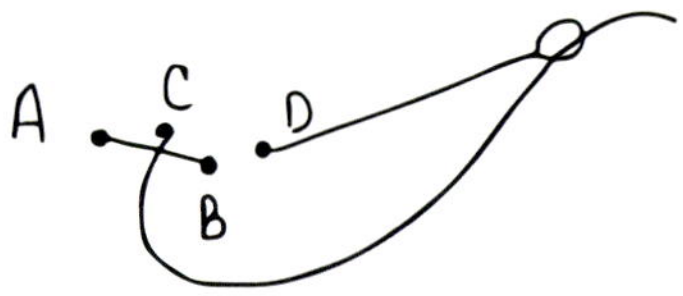

The Stem stitch is an excellent stitch for adding beads and sequins. It handles curves well and is my go-to stitch when outlining an appliquéd piece of fabric. You can add a bead to this in the same way that you would add a bead using the Backstitch.

Bring the needle up at A and down at B, making a slightly diagonal line. Bring the needle up at C (about the middle of your first stitch) and down at D. Continue until you have finished your line.

Threads used in this sampler (from the outside edge to the inside):

DMC Cotton Retors Mat size 4 with size 6 seed beads

Wonderfil Specialty Threads, perle cotton size 8 & size 8 seed beads

Rainbow Gallery, Very Velvet

Wonderfil Specialty Threads / Sue Spargo Eleganza perle cotton size 5 with sequins

The Thread Gatherer, Sheeps silk & size 6 seed beads

DMC Tapestry Wool

Wonderfil Specialty Threads, Dazzle & sequins

The Thread Gatherer, Aurora

Rainbow Gallery, Splendor 12-ply silk with size 6 seed beads

Wonderfil Specialty Threads, Dazzle

DMC Cotton Retors Mat

Chain Stitch

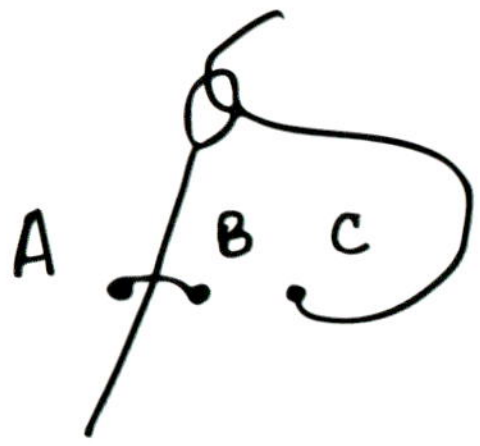

The Chain stitch works well for curves or straight lines. It has a lovely braided appearance when worked in a line. Beads and sequins can be added to the sides of the chain or to the center of each chain. Play around with this stitch and a few beads on your practice hoop and see what combinations you can create.

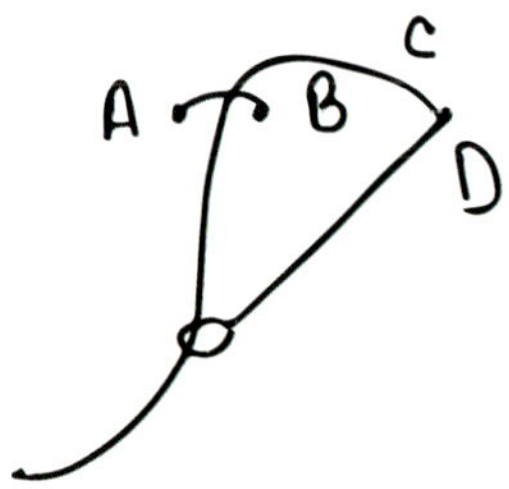

Make a small Backstitch from A to B. Bring your needle up at C and slip it under the Backstitch. Bring the needle down at D. Continue this stitch by going under both threads of each previous Chain stitch.

Threads used in this sampler (from the outside edge to the inside):

DMC Cotton Retors Mat size 4

Wonderfil Specialty Threads, perle Cotton size 8 and size 8 seed beads

DMC Tapestry Wool and size 32 seed beads

The Thread Gatherer, Aurora & size 6 seed beads

Rainbow Gallery, Silk Lame Braid

Weeks Dye Works, size 3 pearl cotton

Wonderfil Specialty Threads / Sue Spargo, Eleganza perle Cotton size 8 and sequins

Rainbow Gallery, Petite Very Velvet

Wonderfil Specialty Threads / Sue Spargo, Eleganza perle cotton size 3 and size 6 seed beads

Wonderfil Specialty Threads, Dazzle

Hungarian Braided Chain Stitch

Much like the Chain stitch, the Hungarian Braided Chain stitch works into a much thicker line. When you want a substantial stitch for stems of vines, this is definitely the stitch to use. You can add beads in the same way that you would with the Chain stitch. To achieve a line that really stands out, check out the threads that I used and choose a thicker thread for this stitch.

Make a small backstitch from A-B. Bring your needle up at C and slip it under the backstitch. Bring your needle down at C.

Bring the needle up at D and take the needle and thread under the original anchor stitch (A-B). Bring the needle back down through D and do not pull the thread all the way through the fabric.

Bring the needle up at E and take the needle and thread under the original Chain stitch. The needle will be sitting on top of the loose Chain stitch. While the needle is resting on the loose Chain stitch, pull the thread to tighten the stitch. Then pull the needle through, but again do not tighten the thread. Bring your needle up at F. It will now sit on top of the loose Chain stitch as it goes under the previous Chain stitch. Pull the thread tight and then pull the needle and thread completely through the Chain stitch, without pulling the thread completely tight.

Continue in this same way until your chain has been finished. Each Chain stitch will interlock with the previous Chain stitch, which creates a heavily chained row of stitches.

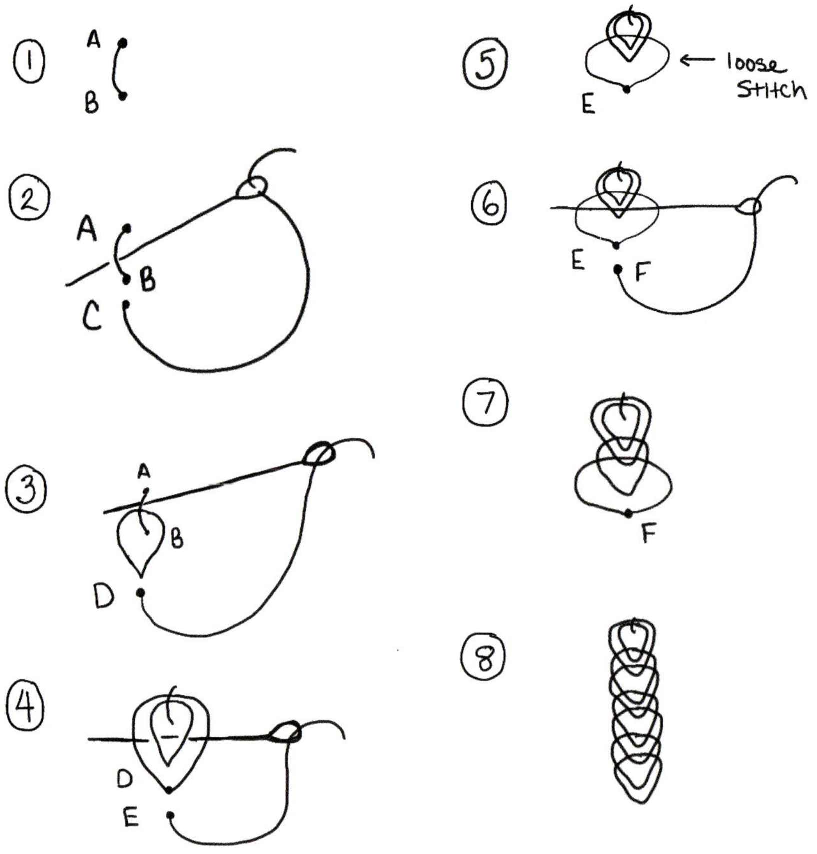

Threads used in this sampler (from the outside edge to the inside):

Wonderfil Specialty Threads / Sue Spango, Eleganza perle cotton size 5
Weeks Dye Works, pearl cotton 3
DMC Cotton Retors Mat size 4 & size 8 seed beads
Wonderfil Specialty Threads, Dazzle
Rainbow Gallery, Rainbow Tweed
DMC Tapestry Wool
Wonderfil Specialty Threads / Sue Spango, Eleganza perle cotton size 3
The Thread Gatherer, Silk 'n Colors
Wonderfil Specialty Threads / Spargo Eleganza perle 5
Wonderfil Specialty Threads, perle cotton size 8

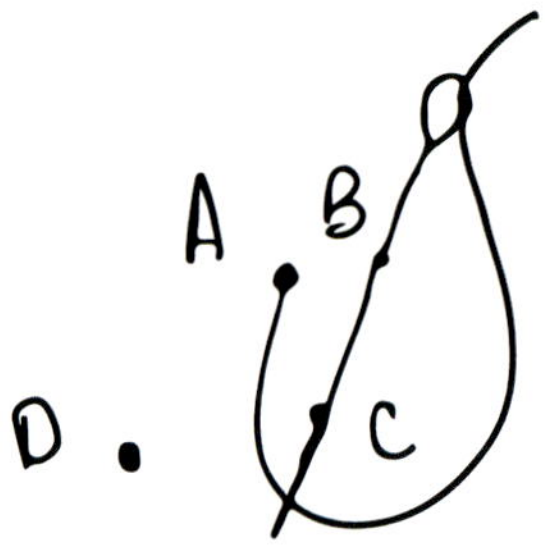

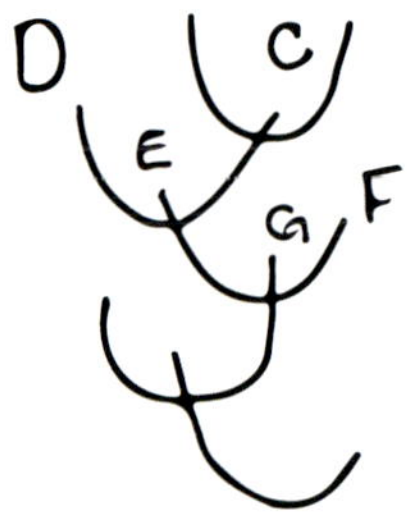

Feather Stitch

The Feather stitch is an open Chain stitch. This stitch is worked from top to bottom and is an excellent choice to use for vines or stems.

Bring the needle up at A and down at B. Do not pull the thread all the way through at B. Bring the needle back up at C to form a 'U' shape. Then bring the needle down at D. Before pulling the thread all the way through, bring the needle back up at E. Repeat until you have your desired length.

Threads used in this sampler (from the outside edge to the center):

Wonderfil Specialty Threads, perle cotton size 8 and size 8 seed beads

Wonderfil Specialty Threads / Sue Spargo, Eleganza perle cotton size 3

Wonderfil Specialty Threads, Dazzle & size 6 seed beads

Weeks Dye Works, size 8 pearl cotton and sequins

Rainbow Gallery, Rainbow Tweed

The Thread Gatherer, silk 'n colors and size 11 seed beads

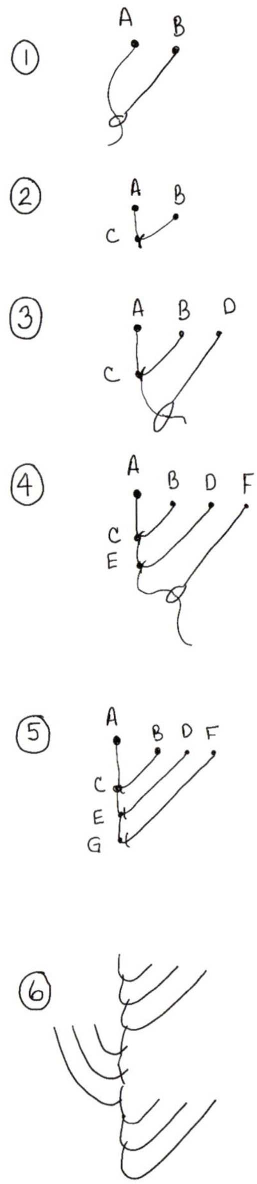

Maidenhair Stitch

The Maidenhair stitch is worked the same as the Feather stitch, however rather than alternating from side-to-side, you will work three stitches then alternate to the opposite side and work three more stitches and back again to repeat. It is a decorative stitch that can pair well with other stitches like the Colonial Knot and Lazy Daisies. A bead can be added to each "feather" of the stitch.

Bring the needle up at A and down at B without taking the thread all the way through the fabric. Bring the needle up at C to secure that stitch.

Bring the needle down at D, again not pulling the thread all the way through. I catch the thread with my thumb at this point to remind me not to pull it through! Secure the stitch by bringing the needle and thread up at E.

Bring the needle down at F and up at G to finish the stitches on the right. Continue this same pattern to complete the stitches on the left side of the middle stitches.

Threads used in this sampler (from the outside edge to the center):

Wonderfil Specialty Threads, perle cotton size 8
DMC Cotton Retors Mat size 4
Wonderfil Specialty Threads, Dazzle
The Thread Gatherer, Silken Pearl and size 8 seed beads
Weeks Dye Works, pearl cotton size 3
Weeks Dye Works, pearl cotton size 8 and size 8 seed beads
Wonderfil Specialty Threads / Sue Spargo, Eleganza perle cotton size 3

Wheatear Stitch

While I have this stitch listed in the line section, you'll notice in the sampler that it can also be stitched as an isolated stitch. It is a flexible stitch that works just as well on a border as it does as an accent stitch.

Begin with a small stitch, bringing your needle up at A and down at C. The next stitch will come up at B and down at C.

Bring your thread up at D and slide it underneath the 'V' that you just made, bringing the needle and thread back down at D. This is a single Wheatear stitch.
To continue making a line, bring your thread up at E and down at F, which is where your previous stitch ended, up at G and down at F. Continue until you have your desired length of stitches.

Threads used in this sampler (from the outside edge to the inside)
DMC Cotton Retors Mat size 4
Wonderfil Specialty Threads, perle cotton size 8
The Thread Gatherer, Silken Pearl and size 8 seed beads
The Thread Gatherer Sheep's Silk and size 6 seed beads
Weeks Dye Works, pearl cotton size 8 and size 10 seed beads
Wonderfil Specialty Threads / Sue Spango, Eleganza perle cotton size 3
Wonderfil Specialty Threads, perle cotton size 8 and sequins
Rainbow Gallery, Silk Lame Braid and sequins

Embroidery Fill Stitches

Woven Filling Stitch

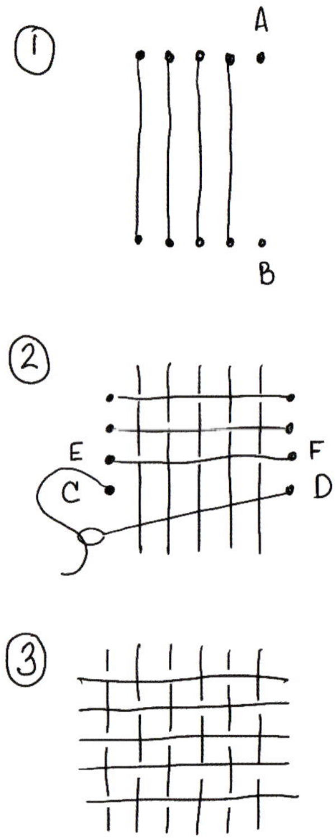

This stitch can fill large areas with texture. It is versatile and works just as well for square shapes as it does for circles or leaves. This is a stitch for which I recommend the use of a tapestry needle, because the threads are woven and a tapestry needle does not have a sharp end to catch the threads while you are weaving.

Bring your needle up at A and down at B to create your first vertical stitch. Continue creating vertical stitches like so, until your area has been filled. You have just created your foundation stitches.

With your weaving thread, bring your needle up at C and down at D going over and under each of the vertical foundation stitches. Your next horizontal row of stitches will also go over and under the foundation stitches but opposite your C-D row. For instance, if you began stitching by going over and under and over and under, then your next row will begin by going under then over then under then over (as illustrated in the third drawing). It sounds more complicated than it actually is! Just remember with each new row to do the opposite of your previous row. (If you are familiar with weaving, this will seem perfectly natural to you!)

Continue until you have finished weaving your shape.

Threads used in this sampler (from top to bottom, left to right):

The Thread Gatherer, Silk 'n Colors
The Thread Gatherer, Silken Pearl
Rainbow Gallery, Rhapsody
DMC Tapestry Wool
The Thread Gatherer, Aurora
Weeks Dye Works, pearl Cotton size 3
Rainbow Gallery, Very Velvet
Wonderfil Specialty Threads, perle cotton size 8
DMC Cotton Retors Mat, size 4

Fishbone Stitch

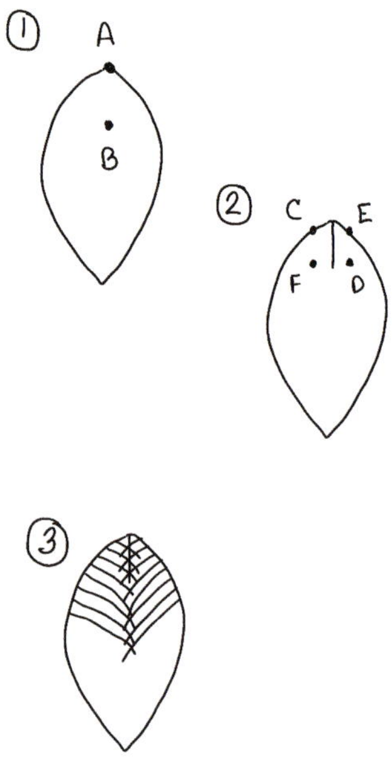

This stitch works best on a teardrop or leaf shape, so it makes an excellent choice when stitching botanical pieces. It can be helpful to draw a center line down your shape with a chalk pencil, or just envision an imaginary center line as you stitch. This stitch is worked from top to bottom.

Make a straight stitch from A to B in the center of your shape. Your next diagonal stitches will cross over the first stitch line. Bring the needle up at C, down at D then up at E and down at F. Continue forming each stitch like this until you have filled your shape.

Threads used in this sampler (from top to bottom, left to right):

Rainbow Gallery, Very Velvet
Rainbow Gallery, Rainbow Tweed
The Thread Gatherer, Silk 'n Colors
Weeks Dye Works, pearl cotton size 3
Rainbow Gallery, Rhapsody
DMC Tapestry Wool
Wonderfil Specialty Threads, perle cotton size 8 and size 8 beads
DMC Cotton Retors Mat size 4

Cretan Stitch

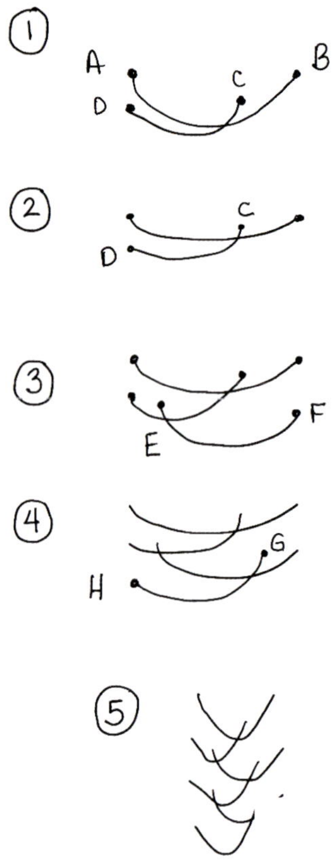

As you stitch the Cretan stitch, you will notice that it can be more open or more closed, depending on how closely each stitch is worked. It also can vary depending on the thread weight that you decide to use. This is a stitch that is reminiscent of the Feather stitch.

Bring the needle up at A and down at B without taking the thread all the way through.

Bring the needle up at C and down at D. Continue by going up at E and down at F. You will be going back and forth this way until you have finished a line or filling in an area.

Threads used in this sampler (from top to bottom, left to right):

Wonderfil Specialty Threads, Dazzle

Wonderfil Specialty Threads / Sue Spargo, Eleganza perle cotton size 5

Wonderfil Specialty Threads, Dazzle

DMC Cotton Retors Mat size 4

Wonderfil Specialty Threads / Sue Spargo, Eleganza perle cotton size 5

DMC Tapestry Wool

Weeks Dye Works, pearl cotton size 3

Wonderfil Specialty Threads / Sue Spargo, Eleganza perle cotton size 3

DMC Cotton Retors Mat size 4

Raised Stem Stitch Band

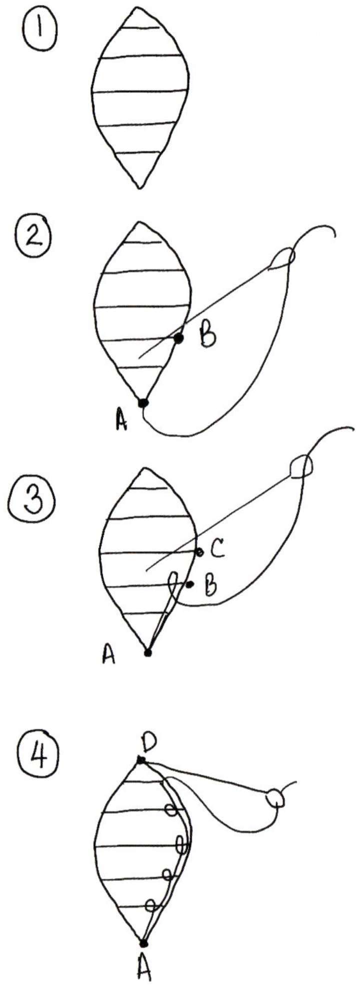

This stitch has a foundation row of straight stitches that are worked from left to right. Once the foundation stitches are down, the remaining stitches will be worked much like the Stem stitch. This stitch allows you to quickly fill an area, although it is a stitch that uses up a lot of thread. It is great for stitching textured leaves.

Work a row of straight stitches horizontally over the shape you want to fill. Working vertically from the bottom of the shape to the top, bring your needle up at A, skip over the first stitch and slide your needle under the second horizontal stitch at B. Pull through. These stitches are all worked above the fabric. Continue working this way, bringing the needle under stitch C and working your way to the top stitches. When you reach the top, bring your needle down through the fabric and start this same process again at the bottom of the shape. Continue until the shape is filled.

Threads used in this sampler (from top to bottom, left to right):
Wonderfil Specialty Threads, perle cotton size 8
Weeks Dye Works, pearl cotton size 3
Wonderfil Specialty Threads, Dazzle
DMC cotton Retors Mat size 4
Rainbow Gallery, very velvet
The Thread Gallery, Aurora
Wonderfil Specialty Threads / Sue Spargo, Eleganza perle cotton size 3
DMC Tapestry Wool

Fly Stitch

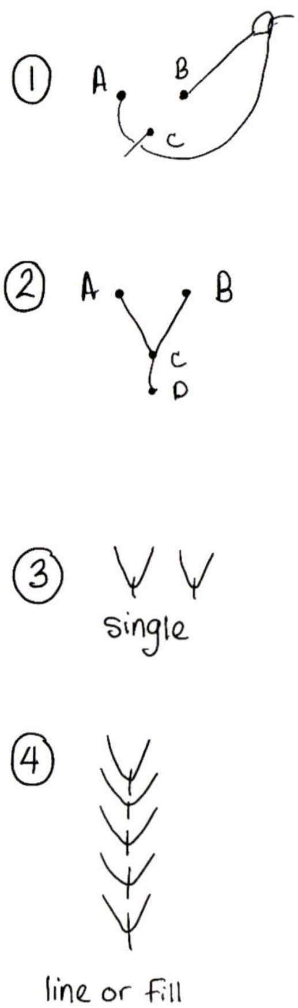

Although this stitch falls into the category of filling stitches, it can also be worked as an isolated stitch to add detail to your embroidery. It is a simple stitch and beads can be added to the center to create a lovely beaded line on a filled shape.

Bring the needle up at A, then down at B and diagonally up at C. The needle should be on top of the thread as you pull it through. Bring it down at D to secure the stitch. You have just made an isolated Fly stitch. To use the Fly stitch to fill a shape, continue working each new stitch close to the previous stitch in the same manner.

Threads used in this sampler (from top to bottom, left to right):
The Thread Gatherer, silken pearl
DMC Cotton Retors Mat size 4 and size 8 seed beads
Wonderfil Specialty Threads / Sue Spargo, Eleganza perle cotton size 3
Wonderfil Specialty Threads, Dazzle
Weeks Dye Works, pearl cotton size 3
DMC Tapestry Wool
Wonderfil Specialty Threads, perle cotton size 8
Rainbow Gallery, Very Velvet
The Thread Gatherer, Sheep's silk

Isolated Embroidery Stitches

Lazy Daisy

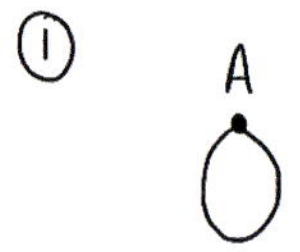

Lazy daisies can be stitched as single stitches or they can be sewn as multiples, as in a flower shape. Beads can be added to the side of the petal or to the center. Play around with adding beads to see what variety you can create!

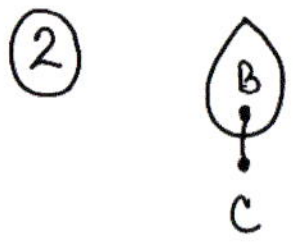

Bring your needle and thread up at A and then back down through A but do not pull the thread all the way through. Secure this stitch by bringing your needle up at B and then down at C. This is your first petal.

Threads used in this sampler (from the outside edge to the inside):

DMC Cotton Rotors Mat size 4 and Sue Spargo Eleganza perle cotton size 5

The Thread Gatherer, Silk 'n Colors and size 8 seed beads

DMC Tapestry Wool

Rainbow Gallery, Very Velvet

The Thread Gatherer, Aurora

Wonderfil Specialty Threads / Sue Spargo, Eleganza perle cotton size 3 and size 6 seed beads

Wonderfil Specialty Threads, Dazzle

Rainbow Gallery, Sparkle Rays

Colonial Knot

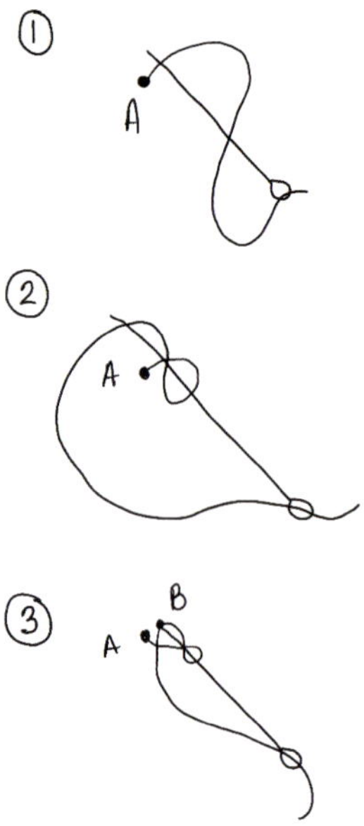

Colonial Knots are my favorite type of knot and can quickly be worked once you practice the basic movement of creating the stitch. They are my preferred alternative to the French Knot and can be used in the same way. If you want to add sequins or larger beads to your work, this is a great stitch to use with them.

Bring your needle and thread up through the fabric at A. Hold the thread so that it looks like a backward letter C and place the needle in the middle of the C shape. The needle remains there while you twist the thread up and over the needle and then below the needle. This will look like a figure 8. Keep the tension on the thread while you insert your needle at B and pull the needle and thread through the fabric. This is your first Colonial Knot.

Threads used in this sampler (from the outside edge to the inside):
DMC Cotton Retors Mat size 4
The Thread Gatherer, Silken Pearl
DMC Tapestry wool
Wonderfil Specialty Threads / Sue Spargo, Eleganza perle cotton size 3 and sequins
Rainbow Gallery, Rainbow Tweed
The Thread Gatherer, Aurora
Koigu KPPPM needlepoint yarn & sequins
Wonderfil Specialty Threads, perle cotton size 8
Weeks Dye Works, pearl cotton size 8 & size 11 seed beads
Weeks Dye Works, pearl cotton size 3
Wonderfil Specialty Threads, Dazzle
Wonderfil Specialty Threads, perle cotton size 8

Cross Stitch

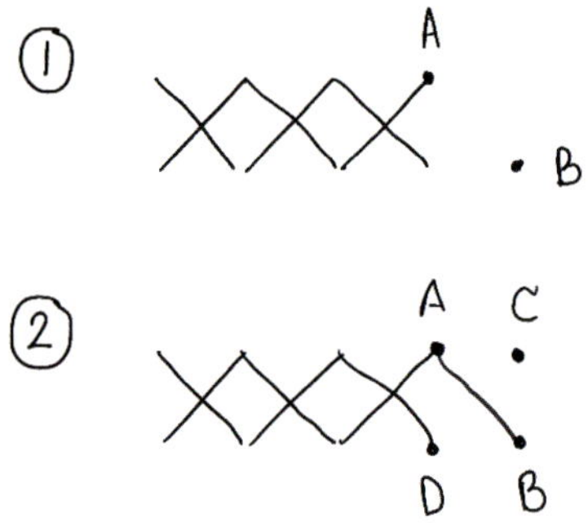

Traditionally, this stitch is used on a countable fabric called Aida cloth for Cross stitch. Stitches in counted Cross stitch are uniform in size and are worked with a pattern to create a design. When using them in embroidery, they can be worked in a line or scattered individually throughout your stitching.

Bring the needle up at A and down at B. Bring the needle up again at C and down at D to complete the first stitch.

Threads used in this sampler (from the outside edge to the inside):

Wonderfil Specialty Threads / Sue Spargo, Eleganza perle cotton size 5

DMC Cotton Retors Mat size 4

Weeks Dye Works, pearl cotton size 3 & size 8 seed beads

Weeks Dye Works, pearl cotton size 8

The Thread Gatherer, Aurora

The Thread Gatherer, Silk 'n Colors

Rainbow Gallery, Rainbow Tweed

Wonderfil Specialty Threads / Sue Spargo, Eleganza perle cotton size 5

Raised Cup Stitch

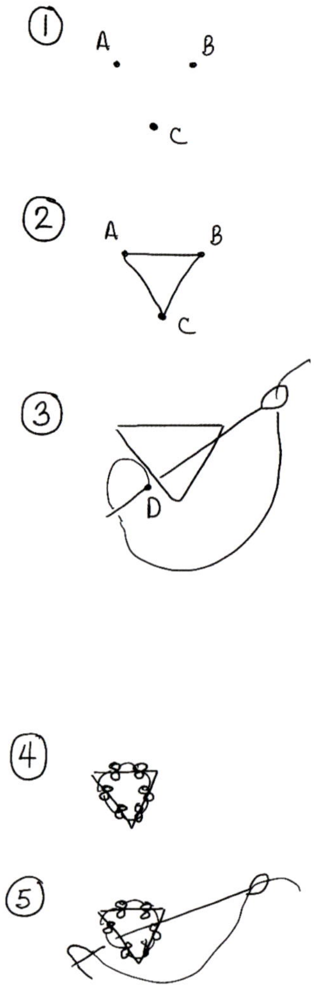

This is a beautiful dimensional stitch that allows you to add depth to your embroidery. Adding a bead in the center of this stitch is a fun way to nestle a little sparkle to your work! This is a woven stitch and it is worked above the fabric, so a tapestry needle should be used to avoid catching threads with the sharp point of a needle.

Create a triangle by bringing your needle up at A, down at B, up at C and down at B, up again at A and down again at C. Once these foundation stitches have been made, all of the other stitches will be woven (using the foundation stitches) on top of the fabric.

Bring the needle up at D and slide the needle under the foundation stitch. Your thread will form a "C" shape. Take the needle through the C and pull all the way through. Repeat this same step until you have two stitches on each side of the triangle foundation stitches.

Your next row will be stitched the same way. This time, you will be going under the thread between the two knots that you just created on each side of the triangle. When you have worked your way around the triangle, simply take your needle and thread through the fabric at any point in the triangle. You will notice that your stitches are slightly loose and this will allow you to gently shape them so that they resemble a round cup shape. When I do this, I just use my needle to arrange each stitch in place. You can leave it as is or add a bead to the center like you can see in my sampler.

Threads used in this sampler (from the outside edge to the center):

The Thread Gatherer, Silken Pearl
Wonderfil Specialty Threads / Sue Spargo, Eleganza perle cotton size 3 & size 6 seed beads
Weeks Dye Works, pearl cotton 3 & size 6 seed beads
DMC Cotton Retors Mat 4 and size 32 seed beads

Algerian Eye Stitch

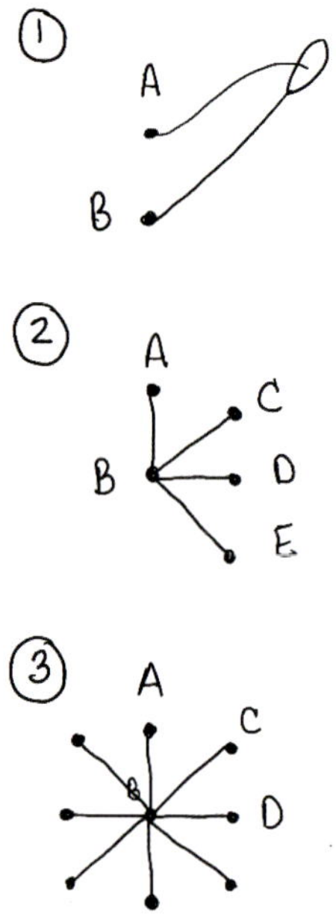

Much like the Cross stitch, the Algerian Eye stitch is found in counted work, like needlepoint. However, it is an excellent addition to free-form embroidery. It is a simple stitch that can add detail to botanical embroidery.

Bring the needle up at A and down at B. Every other stitch that you make will also go through the fabric at B. Bring your needle up at C then down at B, up at D then down at B, up at E then down at B. Continue in this way until you have stitched all of the spokes.

Threads used in this sampler (from the outside edge to the center):

The Thread Gatherer, sheep's silk
Weeks Dye Works, pearl cotton size 8
Wonderfil Specialty Threads, perle cotton size 8
Weeks Dye Works, pearl cotton size 3
Wonderfil Specialty Threads / Sue Spargo, Eleganza perle cotton size 3

Bullion Knot

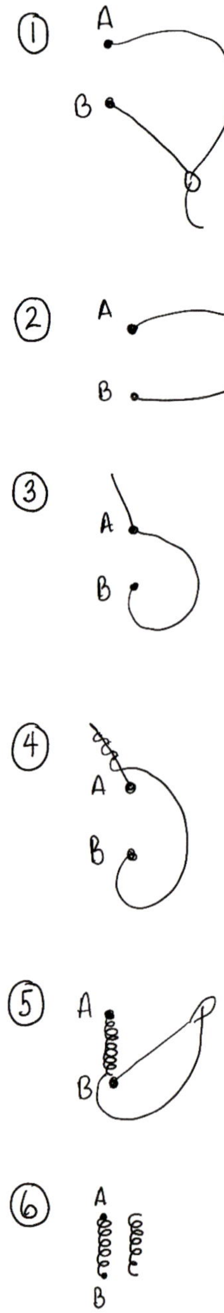

The Bullion Knot is a wrapped stitch that can have a varied appearance depending on the type of thread you use and the way you work the stitch. It can sit flat on the fabric or it can be raised. It can stay in a straight line or it can be worked into a curve. It is a really fun stitch to embroider!

To do this stitch, you will need a Milliners needle. Because you will be wrapping the threads around the needle, the shaft of the needle needs to be the same thickness from top to bottom.

Bring the needle up at A and then down at B, but do not pull the thread all the way through. Take the needle back up at A but do not bring it all the way through. Using the thread from A, wrap it around the needle until you are able to lay your needle down from A to B and have enough stitches to fill that area. Holding the stitches that are wrapped around the needle, gently pull the needle and thread through the wrapped stitches. Take the needle down through B, securing the stitches.

Threads used in this sampler (from the outside edge to the inside):

Wonderfil Specialty Threads / Sue Spargo, Eleganza perle cotton size 5

DMC Cotton Retors Mat size 4 with size 8 seed beads

Anchor / Coats & Clark, Stranded Cotton

Weeks Dye Works, pearl cotton size 3

Wonderfil Specialty Threads / Sue Spargo, Eleganza perle cotton size 3

The Thread Gatherer, Silk 'n Colors

CHAPTER TWO

Exploring Fabric Collage

My first two books focused on fabric collage with embroidery. I wanted to revisit that technique here, because it is how I started my embroidery process and it is a method that I still use when creating projects.

Before I began embroidering, I was into scrapbooking. Much like quilters and crafters love walking through a fabric store and looking at all of the different fabrics, I loved walking through my local scrapbooking store, (which sadly doesn't exist anymore), and looking at all of the different papers. There were so many possibilities I felt I could create, just by cutting up paper and layering it with other pieces of paper. Today I get that same feeling when I look at a pile of fabrics. It feels like the creative possibilities are endless!

NEEDLES DOWN!

Out with the Victorian, in with the Collage!

How are the world wide web and collage art alike? Both were thought to be a passing phase; a novelty form of art that would not be around for long.

The art of collage had its beginnings in the Modernist period. As artists were eschewing the Victorian time period, deeming its art and traditions obsolete, new forms began to take the place of more traditional art. Experimental art that represented the time of war and industrialization encouraged a newfound creativity with materials and techniques. Collage was one of these techniques, soon made popular by artists like Pablo Picasso and Georges Braque. Both of these artists experimented with adding pieces of paper and objects to their artwork. Being truly mixed-media, these artworks were combinations of paint and any other object deemed worthy of being considered art. Art movements, such as Surrealism, began to include collage in their work, making photomontages, a combination of photos and paper with words. Clearly, not just a novelty art form, collage could soon be found in every area of art...including textile arts!

Textile collage can be both two or three dimensional, photo realistic or abstract, simple or complicated. From crazy quilts to hoops to sculptures made from fabric, collage finds its way into every area of art. It continues to remain a very popular art form, accessible to every level of artist.

Supplies

Let's get right to the supplies that you'll need to get yourself started in fabric collaging.

Fabric

The reason I love smaller scale embroidery projects is that not a lot of fabric is needed to get started. You will not use yards of fabric on one piece, unless you are making a large-scale project! In fact, getting started with a few fat quarter cuts of fabric is both feasible and what I always suggest.

When looking for fabric, the number one rule is: choose what you love! That's it. There are no other rules. If you love it, you will enjoy working with it. Embroidery is a slow, take-your-time sort of craft. There is no rushing the process. It will only go as fast as your hands can stitch and you will be sitting with the fabric that you chose for quite a long while. This is part of what I find so soothing about embroidery.

You do not need to limit yourself to only quilting cotton. There are beautiful fabrics that are textured, silky, rough, lacy – and they can all be used in your projects. Once, at a shop in the Fashion District in NYC, a kind shopkeeper gave me a bag of scraps when I told him about what I do with fabric. The array of textures in that one bag served me well for years. So, remember that what one crafter, quilter, fashion designer or upholsterer throws away, may be an embroiderer's best friend. Be resourceful!

Iron and Fusibles

An iron is essential to fabric appliqué because the heat of the iron helps the fusible to adhere to the fabric. You can use any iron for this purpose. My personal favorite is the Oliso® Mini Project Iron. It is small enough to iron tiny pieces without taking over my workspace. I do not set up an ironing board when I am working. Instead, I use a Project Wool Felted Quilting Mat that I set up on my desk. Because my studio is quite small, I like being able to have everything easily accessible on my desk. This iron and the pressing mat are my perfect appliqué combination!

I use Therm-o-Web's HeatnBond Lite™ as my main adhesive. When you open a package of this, you will notice that it has a paper-like side and a shiny side. When adhering the HeatnBond, follow the steps (Page 81). You can purchase the HeatnBond by the yard at a fabric store or in a package. Because it is the only fusible I use, I buy yards of it and always have it on hand!

Create a Fabric Collage

Using the hoop as a guide, place it on the fabric and cut out the fabric shape. Leave yourself several inches of extra space all the way around the hoop.

Place the fabric on an ironing board or mat and iron the fabric.

Secure the fabric inside of the hoop and set it aside until later.

Cut a section of the appliqué fabric. Make sure that the pieces you want to appliqué are included in this section of the fabric. Depending on what you are appliquéing, you may have one or more fabric sections when you have finished this step.

Iron the sections of fabric that you just cut out.

Unpackage the fusible. I will be using the HeatnBond Lite.

Place the wrong side of the fabric on top of the shiny side of the HeatnBond.

Cut the fusible into the shape of your fabric.

Iron the Fabric to the HeatnBond. Make sure that you are not placing your iron on any shiny parts of the fusible because it will adhere to your iron and make a mess!

Now that the fusible has been attached, use your scissors to cut the desired pieces for appliquéing. The fine details do not need to be cut yet.

Once the small appliqué pieces have been cut from the fabric, finely cut the detail pieces. Peel the paper backing from them.

Bring the background fabric back and take it out of the hoop. The shape of the hoop will be impressed onto the fabric. Arrange the appliqué pieces within that impression.

When the pieces have been arranged, iron them into place.

Re-situate the fabric back in its original position inside the hoop and you are now ready to embroider your piece!

Let's Look at Fabric Appliqué in Action!

Fabric Appliqué Wall Hanging

Many of the projects that I create are stitched in, and remain in, an embroidery hoop. This is a completely different project and one that allowed me to experiment with other methods of fabric appliqué.

You will notice when I give directions for fabric collage, I usually recommend using an adhesive, like HeatnBond, to adhere the fabric pieces together before the embroidery process begins. This wall hanging was created using a different method, which makes the end result feel like a well-worn quilt or garment. The adhesive that I chose to use is something that you probably have hanging around in your office supplies: a washable glue stick. Yes, you can use washable glue to adhere fabric together before stitching it!

I began this piece with a fat quarter cut of fabric, complete with the selvage edge intact. I have already mentioned how sewing with a machine is not my go-to activity and the same goes for measuring fabric! If I can get away with not using exact measurements, then I will always choose that method. So I decided to adhere all of my fabric appliqué on top of one fat quarter.

With the fabric facing right side up, I laid in place the pieces that I wanted to appliqué.The size of the pieces did not matter, because I was focusing on color, so each piece was cut to a different size. Before I placed a piece of fabric down, I lightly ran my glue stick on the reverse side of the fabric piece and then I pressed it in place.

Working this way allowed me to pick from my fabrics as I went along and I did not spend much time deliberating over my fabric choices. I then cut out larger pieces to appliqué, such as the moth, bird and flowers scattered throughout. I used the same method of placing each piece down with a touch of glue on the reverse side, to hold it in place. Once everything was in place, I used the Running stitch to embroider straight lines horizontally across this piece. The Blanket stitch was used around the edges and a beaded tassel was secured to the bottom with the same stitch.

This glue stick method does allow for more fraying than you would see if you used a fabric adhesive. I wanted this to have the appearance of a garment or blanket that is well-loved, so the fraying works for this piece. Also this is not a piece that I will be washing in the laundry, so the fraying that is here will not become more pronounced over time.

You can use this method to attach fabric to clothing, making fabric patches. Ensure that you always have the embroidery be the final step of the process. The embroidery stitches are what keeps the appliqué attached to your fabric. As I said, a garment will get a lot of wear and washing, so expect more fraying than you see here. This method allows for a less stiff fabric patch and so it would work well on a pair of worn jeans or a soft flannel.

Embroidery hoops come in all shapes and sizes.

If you want to jazz up your embroidery, try using a triangle or oval or square hoop.

If you have always used wood hoops and want a different look on your finished piece, try a plastic hoop that matches your work.

If you prefer working with wood hoops (like I do!), try painting or staining your hoop. You can also wrap it with a thin strip of fabric or ribbon.

There are so many possibilities if you want to elevate the look of your embroidery hoop!

Simple Fabric Collage

Your first fabric collage (or even your twentieth fabric collage!) does not need to be complicated to still have a visual impact.

This piece of embroidery instantly stands out because of the square-shaped hoop. I originally hooped this piece up in a round hoop. When I added the luna moth to the collage, the round shape of the hoop couldn't accommodate the collage without it looking too overcrowded or too spacious. Enter the square hoop! As soon as I switched to that hoop, the piece instantly looked like a finished piece... and that was without any embroidery!

I chose to keep this piece simple, because within the fabric glass cloche, there is a lot going on. Between the floral background fabric and the colorful mushrooms and plants, I didn't feel much else was necessary to complete the collage. Also, I do not believe that fabric collage is necessarily overwhelming or that it is a craft only for someone who has a keen eye for design.

For fabric collage to feel accessible to everyone, I wanted to show what you can do with just two pieces of fabric. This piece has a single background fabric and then the glass cloche and moth are both cut from a separate piece. In all, just two pieces of fabric are needed for this project. Begin with a simple project like this and then allow yourself the time to focus on the process of the appliqué, fussy cutting and embroidery.

This simple collage also allows the background fabric to be a part of the finished piece, so be sure to choose a fabric that you love. Because it is not covered up with other layers, it is able to stand out and your stitching then ties everything together and makes it feel like a cohesive work of art.

Multi-layered Fabric Collage

When you hear fabric collage, you might envision a piece like this: a background fabric as the base and then lots of layers to make up the collage. My pieces have slowly evolved over the years and have become multi-layered with lots going on within. My process for creating a multi-layered versus a simple collage is exactly the same, every time.

Begin by choosing your background fabric. Place the fabric in the hoop, leaving an extra two-inches around the outside. Set it aside; this is your canvas. From the remaining fabric, cut out the pieces to be appliquéd and apply HeatnBond to each one. Before arranging these appliqués on your canvas, fussy cut each one. This is now the time to arrange and rearrange your pieces until you feel you have created the perfect collage.

To layer a piece like this, first peel off the backing from the fabric sticker that was created above, and iron the HeatnBond to the fabric. Do not iron anything into place just yet. Having the paper backing already peeled off, allows you to iron your pieces into place when the time comes, without disrupting your arrangement. It also allows you to change your mind! Finally, you can remove the background fabric from the hoop and carefully iron the piece as a whole, or you can iron it piece by piece. If you are ironing it as a whole, do not just press the iron on the fabric and hope for the best. Pieces can shift in this process and so it is best to iron section by section until everything is in place. Then you can give the piece one more quick pass with the iron to make sure that everything is secured in place.

Unless you have used very thick fabrics, you should not have a difficult time embroidering through several layers of fabric collage pieces. In this project, there are five layers in the center of the hoop that I stitched through. When stitching through several layers like that, it is best to use a thicker needle to minimize the risk of breaking your needle as you are pulling it through the fabric.

Remember, you do not need to have embroidery covering every piece of fabric in a collage.

Notice on the blue flowers that there are bits of embroidery but there is no stitching on the edges. There are sections that I left unembroidered.

As long as you have some stitching on every fabric piece, you do not need to worry about the applique peeling off of the fabric.

HeatnBond is permanent but only to a point and it can peel off from the fabric over time. Having some embroidery on every piece, secures it and allows it to remain on your work of art.

CHAPTER THREE

Exploring Beading and Embellishing

You know the people who get giddy with excitement when the school supplies begin to show up in stores in the early summertime? And we're not talking giddy because it is soon time for the kids to be heading back to school, but giddy with the excitement of buying new pens and pencils and office supplies. I am one of those people. I get that same giddiness when I walk into a craft store and come face to face with a wall of beads.

Beading Supplies

So let's talk about what you'll need to get started with beading.

As with unembellished embroidery, you will need an embroidery hoop, fabric, thread, scissors and needles. Refer back to Chapter 1 to help you decide what you need to have in your stitching toolbox.

Bead Trays are triangular shaped and can be made of plastic or metal. They are helpful when you are able to set them on a surface and pour into them the variety of beads that you need for a project. I always keep a few bead trays handy to make beading easier.

An awl is a notion that I find very useful in beading (Page 125). It has a sharp point that allows you to make a small hole in the fabric. Certain stitches, like eyelets, begin with a small hole and the awl will help you with that too. It is also useful when adding shank buttons, which require a small hole in the fabric to help them lie flat.

Now, for the part you've all been waiting for. . . the beads! And sequins! And embellishments!

Beads

Let's begin with seed beads, because these are the main types of bead that I use in my embroidery. There are two types: Japanese seed beads and Czech seed beads and both are made of glass. The two are different in that Japanese seed beads have a taller shape and are more uniform in size while Czech seed beads are rounder and can vary in shape. Beads are sized numerically and the smaller the number, the larger the bead. Size 2 beads will be much larger than size 11. (Bead size 32 is the only exception to this rule. These beads are large, and so is their number!) My favorite bead company is John Bead and you can find their beads in square and round tubes at larger craft and fabric stores or online.

Super Duo® beads are a type of Czech bead and they are slightly elongated and have two holes. Further on in this chapter, you will see the oval kitty hoop which was stitched with lots of Super Duo beads. There are such a variety of ways that these can be stitched to the fabric. They can be stitched flat, as on the kitty hoop, or they can be attached in large groups with just one hole, to give a textured, more dimensional appearance.

Czech beads can be found in a large variety of shapes. They can be round, triangular, square, diamond or oval. They can be in a tube as are bugle beads, or they can be shaped like flowers. They can have fun names like Farfalles or Pips. They can be fire-polished, matte, or metallic. Essentially, you could stitch using only Czech beads and your work would have endless variety.

Another type of bead is an accent bead. When you are in a craft store, these are usually found hanging, strung in long rows. I look for accent beads that are glass or semi-precious stone. I tend to shy away from plastic beads because I like the weight and look of glass and stone beads.

Sequins

I consider sequins to be an embroidery essential! They come in a variety of sizes and can be flat or faceted. I like to add them when my project needs a little bit of shine or sparkle. They can be layered with beads or with stitches on top.

Embellishments

Embellishments are anything which is 2D or 3D that you add to your embroidery. Buttons, beads, charms, paper, ribbon, photographs, the list can go on and on and is only limited by whether you can attach it to your project!

I like to look for embellishments at my local craft and fabric stores. I do not limit myself to browsing just in the bead aisles, because many great embellishment ideas come from the scrapbooking, stamping and card aisles of the store. I also love to browse thrift shops and antique marketplaces, where I often find interesting and unusual pieces to use in my work.

Tim Holtz is one of my favorite designers and many of the projects that I create use embellishments from his "Idea ology" line.

Beading Thread

Chapter 1 detailed all of the embroidery threads that I use, so refer to that for a more detailed look into embroidery thread.

When I am simply using beads in my stitching, I use Fruitti by Wonderfil Specialty Threads. It is a thin but strong thread that comes in an array of variegated colors. I like to use a thread that matches the beads, even though my intent is not for the thread to be seen. If my thread matches and there are gaps in the beadwork, then no one will be any the wiser!

Embroidery on Printed Fabric with a Central Motif

My love of fabric designs is what first started me on my embroidery journey. I know that I'm not alone in falling in love with fabric and wanting to hold onto it for the perfect project. One of my favorite projects is to use a fabric design that I really love and embroider it, following the lines and adding dimension. The fabric becomes the embroidery pattern.

Embroidering on fabric is as beginner-friendly as you can get! This is a project that can be simple or advanced and that is determined by you, the stitcher. The next few projects will give you ideas on how to begin your own embroidery project on fabric.

A Tale of Two Kitties and Two Beading Methods

The first step in beginning an embroidery project is to find a fabric you really love. It can be helpful to start with a motif as the central focus in your embroidery.

Both of these hoops have a kitty as their central motif. By choosing a fabric with a central design, you are forced to make several decisions as you get started: will the motif be the lead embroidery work or will the background be the focus? Being faced with a decision to make upfront, is helpful as you begin to gather supplies and think through how you want to proceed with the piece.

Notice that I made the decision in the oval kitty hoop to bead only the background and I left the kitty motif entirely un-beaded. By stitching it this way, I was able to create negative space in the center of the hoop. I still wanted the kitty to be the focal point, however, so I chose beads in colors that matched the background fabric. When you choose to match the beads to the fabric, you are creating texture without adding distraction. The beads should not take over the piece, but should blend into the background.

You may be wondering now, what comes first: the beading or the embroidery? Well, every piece is different. In this piece, since I knew there would be no beadwork on the kitty (with the exception of the flower bouquet she is holding), I did all of the embroidery first. I was going to be adding height to the fabric with the beads and so I didn't want to run into the problem of catching my embroidery needle and thread in the beads around her. Then I stitched the tiny size 11 beads into her bouquet. Once my central motif was stitched, I added the beads to the background.

How should I display my embroidery projects?

Embroidery makes an excellent addition to a gallery wall or shelf. A larger hoop can even be hung on a wall by itself (to do this, look for large quilting hoops rather than embroidery hoops).

You can hang the hoop directly on the wall using the hardware of the hoop. Or you can tie a piece of fabric or a ribbon to the hardware and then hang the hoop from that. Get creative and try a variety of methods to display your finished pieces!

My second kitty hoop, Professor Kitty, is a fabric panel created by artist Melissa Averinos. You will see several of her panels throughout the projects in this book! Melissa designed this one to fit perfectly in a 10" square hoop and you can visit her shop to find other fabric designs that are simply perfect for embroidery.

My first step, after putting the fabric inside the hoop, was to decide which method I would use for the embroidery: should I focus on the motif or on the background? Since I already embroidered a kitty hoop with the motif un-beaded, I decided to bead Professor Kitty and leave the background for embroidery.

Deciding which part of the fabric to bead makes it easier for you to select your beads and threads. I chose bead colors to match his outfit and fur colors exactly as they appeared on the fabric. I added one more section of beads to the outer yellow border, and then simply embroidered the rest.

For many of the hoops throughout this book, I have removed the hoop from the project, once the fabric has been tightened and glued to the inner hoop. (you can read more about how to finish your hoop in Chapter 7).

The oval Kitty hoop is an example of this method. Along the outside edge, I glued a silk ribbon, beaded it with large accent beads and then tied a knot at the top to hang it from.

Let Your Embroidery Take Flight: *Blending Beads and Embroidery*

In the previous section we discussed using a fabric with a central motif and then either beading or embroidering that motif. But what if you have a fabric with a motif and you want to use embroidery and beading combined throughout the project?

My two hoops were created using fabric from artist Flora Bowley. This was one of those fabric purchases where you buy a yard, leave the store and end up wishing you had bought the remaining bolt! I just adore everything about this fabric and so I have tried to use every last bit of it sparingly.

I was able to create two hoops out of the fabric that I had remaining, both of which are examples of how to blend both embroidery stitches and beads for a cohesive look throughout a piece. Because they have been subtly combined, neither the beadwork nor the embroidery stands out by itself. It is a delicate balance to keep when you are embroidering a piece like this.

Decide what features you want to highlight on your fabric. I loved the blend of colors in the sky on the round hoop, and so I used lots of Straight stitches in a very thin thread to accent it, without making it the focus.

Adding embellishments, like sequins, to the body of the bird gives it a shimmer, even from a distance.

The second hoop has the same color palette, being cut from the same piece of fabric. But here, I chose to emphasize different parts of the fabric.

In this piece, I ignored the color of the sky and stitched over it in a subtle blend of clear and white and silver bugle beads. The beads added sparkle but didn't overwhem the rest of the piece.

When I embroider a piece without putting the emphasis on either the motif or the background, many of the decisions that I make are done in an organic way, as I am working.

I do not begin with a plan on how to proceed before I start the project. As I sit with it and stitch, I am thinking ahead to the next step, but not the next five steps.

I slowly ruminate on ideas as I stitch and the piece comes together in this way.

Being able to work like this is an excellent next step in your embroidery process!

To complement the other hoop, I used some of the same colors in the bird but chose to add more beadwork to the black in the bottom half of the hoop.

Encrusted Embroidery on Printed Fabric

Encrusted embroidery is exactly what it sounds like: layering and nestling embroidery stitches together, so they completely cover an area. Many examples of encrusted embroidery are worked in a very simple color palette, such as a piece worked all in white. But, as you can tell from my previous projects, I love color! For me, life is too short to keep a minimal color palette! So, this will be a lesson on how to create an encrusted embroidery piece, packed with color.

This hoop is made with an Anna Maria Horner print that I love. I always suggest that you pick a fabric to work with that you enjoy looking at. An encrusted embroidery project is time consuming, so invest time up-front looking for a design that you love! If you pick a piece of fabric that you only kind of like, you might find that your excitement to work on your project fizzles out before you finish.

With a project like this, determine the size based on what part of your fabric and by how much of that fabric you want to see in your finished project. If you love an entire piece of fabric, but know that you get overwhelmed by big projects, then start small. Begin by choosing a 5" or 7" hoop. Completing this will give you an idea of the amount of time that will be required to finish, when you use a larger sized hoop. This will help you decide if you are ready to tackle something bigger!

When I choose a hoop size, I like to have several available in various shapes and sizes. With these at hand, I can test them against my fabric to determine my best placement of the design. Before I make any cuts into the fabric, I move the hoop around a little. I may even look at it from a distance. As with all my projects, before I stitch anything, I go through all of my supplies and pull together a wide variety of beads, sequins and thread. I may not use everything that I have pulled out, but it gives me options when I sit down to begin planning, arranging and stitching.

In this piece, I picked a design element that repeated several times, to sew first. I chose the green leaves that were scattered throughout, and worked them with an appropriate green thread, using a simple Satin stitch. Beginning to embroider an element, like these repeating green leaves, is a good way to begin tying everything together. When your piece is finished, you want your eye to travel over every part of your work, without stopping to focus on any one piece that stands out.

I next chose to stitch a larger element with beads, namely, the green beaded plant near the top. Again, at the end of the project you do not want one section to stand out. So with this piece, I had to scatter shine throughout the hoop. This large beaded section could have looked off balance if I had also beaded the pink and red flowers nearby. This is why I limited the main beading to just the plant.

To add shine throughout the hoop, I stitched sequins to the background. I chose sequins that perfectly matched the background fabric so that they did not distract from the rest of the hoop. They added sparkle to balance out the beaded plant, but did not detract from the finished piece.

At this point, I set down my piece to take a picture of it. When you are unsure of how your piece is balanced or what you should do next, always take a picture on your phone. Looking at it through your camera lens allows you to focus on what is working and what might not be working. Sometimes, I will even pause on a project for a day or so. I'll prop it up in another room so that, as I pass by, I can look at it critically and see what it needs.

I determined that my piece had enough bling and so I focused on adding mostly embroidery to the rest, while sprinkling in a few more beads ---- just because I couldn't resist!

I continued stitching until every remaining part of the fabric was covered with beads, sequins and thread. And then I took a step back and gave myself a pat on the back! This embroidery process did not happen overnight. In fact, this particular project took several weeks to finish, so never feel that you aren't stitching fast enough! Encrusted embroidery allows you to really look at every little bit of the fabric you are working with. Remember, finishing a piece really gives you a sense of accomplishment, no matter how long it takes!

NEEDLES DOWN!

Quilting Brings People Together

Quilting at its simplest can be described as simply stitching together several layers of fabric, whether pieced together or as a whole cloth. Early quilts were made to be utilitarian, useful to keep oneself warm at night. Quilted clothing also existed, usually beautifully embellished. The same uses for quilts exist today. Usually a solitary activity, quilting allows for creativity with fabric and design.

If you are a fan of intricate textile art, any quilt could be considered artwork. Whether made to be used or as something beautiful to look at, it was made with considerable time and effort, and that needs to be appreciated. And this solitary effort could lead to some surprising human connections!

I've always been fascinated by crafts that bring people together, especially the quilting bees of the 1800s. As an introvert by nature, the idea of socializing while actively working on something with my hands, sounds like a welcome blending of two activities. One that I love and the other not so much! No matter how romanticized these events have become throughout time, there is something decidedly cozy about sitting together while stitching something that will become useful when finished.

Perhaps the best way to enjoy quilting as an art form, is to visit a quilting convention. Yes, they exist! If you've ever attended one of these events, you'll see an excitement for the beauty and art of quilted pieces. Whether they tell a story, bring attention to a subject or are just beautifully constructed, quilting brings people together.

Exploring Outside of the Hoop with Art Quilts

So you want to take your embroidery project out of the hoop? A mini art quilt might be just the project for you! I've spoken about my fear of sewing machines and quilting in the past, but what I love about art quilts is that they can be completely hand stitched. They can also be whatever dimensions you want! There is so much freedom in the world of art quilts. I am by no means an expert on these, so this passage will not be about the construction of them. There are a great many good books out there on this, so I will leave that subject to the quilting professionals! But I will give you my tips and tricks to create a project like this on your own.

When I begin to construct a project outside of the hoop, my first decision is to choose a workable size. I like the tangible for this job and keep sturdy pieces of cardboard to use as templates. It also helps me to eyeball a finished size quickly. I held up a 12" x 12" piece of cardboard and it felt like just the right size for this project. When deciding on a size, keep it manageable. Handwork takes time and when you are stitching through many layers, it may take even longer! I suggest starting with pieces 12" and smaller. They will pack a visual punch but can also be easily held while you are stitching.

Once I determine the size of my piece, my next step is to choose a color palette. Choosing the palette and the fabrics that will go into the piece is one of my favorite steps in a new project. It means that I can rummage through my fabric shelves and plan my current project (plus the next 10 projects that I might want to work on afterwards!).

When I begin a project, I typically do not know what the completed piece will look like at the end. The process of pulling fabrics and creating a pile is the process that I go through for every project, whether it is inside or outside a hoop.

As I look at my fabric, I will gravitate towards certain elements in the fabric and then I create a project pile of the fabrics I would like to use. A theme will start to develop from these fabrics.

This part of the process can take a fair amount of time and is not always as easy as pulling the first few pieces of fabric from a stack and working with them. For those who struggle to make decisions, it may be best to silence your inner critic during this process!

Really focus on the colors and fabrics that appeal to you. For myself, I notice that I'm drawn to certain palettes during different times of the year.

For this piece, I had a vintage handkerchief that I knew I wanted to include. The green leaves at the bottom right and left of this piece were once part of a larger handkerchief that I found at an antique store. I have a running list of things that I search for when I visit flea markets and antique stores. Linens, especially with botanical motifs, are at the top of that list.

Along with the handkerchief, I had recently purchased a few new Martha Negley fat quarters and they were the same colors as the handkerchief, so they went into my project pile. The theme of this project began to develop in my mind: I would call it "Secret Garden".

Bright and airy projects during the spring and summer months

Rich and jeweled tone palettes during the fall and winter months.

Because you will be spending so much time with your project, it is important to connect with each piece and make sure that it fits the vibe that you want to create.

Embellishments can be anything dimensional from beads to buttons to sequins to paper pieces to photographs. If you can figure out a way to attach it to your fabric, it counts as an embellishment!

Once I narrow down my fabric selections, it's time to look at each piece of the fabric and decide on the elements that I am going to cut and use. Following the directions in Chapter 2, "Exploring Fabric Collage," I create fusible fabric stickers from the chosen elements in my fabric. I like to have more pieces than I will end up using because I can play around with their arrangement, until I decide upon the one(s) that work.

Before I iron anything to my background fabric, I also pull out my box of embellishments. I say box, but in truth I have boxes of them in my collection!

NEEDLES DOWN!

Sequins: *From King Tut to Meltaway Gelatin*

Sequins, or spangles, are small, lightweight discs with a center hole. Sewn to clothing, they give off a beautiful, sparkly appearance. It's hard to imagine that these discs, commonly found in haute couture, were once made from gelatin!

The word sequin is believed to have originated from the Arabic word for coin, *sikka*. Throughout history, small coins were sewn to clothing. This practice made the garment heavy, much like sequined garments today, but it also had the secondary and perhaps more important purpose of announcing to all around, that they were in the company of a very wealthy person. The more coins, the heavier the garment, the richer the wearer.

When King Tut's tomb was discovered and opened in the early 1920s, both the tomb and his preserved clothing were found to be covered in small gold discs, a very early form of sequins. This Egyptian discovery was very exciting to the fashion world of the twenties.

Victorian fashion and Flappers embraced sequins and began adding them to their garments. First made of metal (too heavy) these sequins soon were made from a lighter-weight gelatin, which reflected light, adding to the excitement and free-spirited raucousness of the times. And then they began to melt. When a garment became hot from touch or wet from the rain, the sequins began to disappear and melt away. Just imagine a heavily sequined garment slowly disappearing in the heat and humidity of a New York City summer evening! Gelatin sequins made way for acetate sequins which made way for the sequins of today ---- usually made of plastic.

If you are in a craft store, don't feel that you have to limit your browsing to just the bead aisles. I find great embellishments in the jewelry, sewing and scrapbooking sections! I like to have a variety of embellishments on hand so that I can mix and match with the fabrics during the process of creating a piece. Beads typically come later in the process and can be added to your project right up to the end. However, it really helps to have the larger items chosen and placed at the beginning of your project.

The iron gates at the bottom of this piece became a focal point early on in the creation of this quilt. A secret garden needs an entrance! This is also an example of thinking outside what is typical for embroidery. I found these gates in the scrapbooking section of my local craft store and knew that I liked them and would use them at some point. So into my embellishment box they went, waiting for this Secret Garden idea to strike.

The clear butterflies were also a scrapbooking purchase, and were made of a thicker-than-paper plastic material.

I liked the fact that they were completely see-through and could also be stitched, much like fabric.

Before stitching the butterflies, I took the time to poke small holes through them using an awl. This made stitching them to the fabric much easier, since I could bring my needle and thread through several layers of fabric and the plastic butterflies. You will find an awl in the leatherworking section of your craft store.

Lighting is important in actual gardens, especially if you want to enjoy them at night, and I wanted to include lighting in my Secret Garden as well. Two lengths of chain were cut and stitched to the background fabric. To mimic the lights, I pulled decorative glass beads from my stash and stitched them to the fabric.

The gates, butterflies and chain "lights" were all added to my project in the beginning, right after the fabric pieces were ironed in place. If you decide to use larger elements like these, it is important to know that they will fit and that they match the look of the piece you are creating.

When creating a project like my Secret Garden, something has to connect everything together. Otherwise the finished project can feel disjointed and scattered. My background is a copper colored satin fabric and so my connecting "piece" has to blend the background with every element on the fabric. I chose to use tiny size 11 copper seed beads, of the same color as the background fabric, to pull each flower, butterfly and leaf together. When choosing your piece to connect everything, you want it to be something that can blend into the background and not distract your eye. As you look at this piece from a distance, the copper beads might not even be noticeable. But when you look closely, you will see that they draw everything together into a cohesive piece. Your eye is not distracted by them, but it completes the piece and makes it feel whole.

Another embellishment (and tool) to have on hand if you are interested in adding to your embellishing repertoire, is chain.

Chain links can be found in the jewelry sec ion of your craft store and I like to have several colors and sizes on hand.

When you buy chain, it will typically come packaged in one long length which allows you to determine how much you need to use. To cut the chain, you will need to have a pair of wire cutters. These are easy to find and are usually located in the jewelry section.

As I suggested earlier, I often take photographs along the way, especially when I create a larger piece like this. Seeing a project through the lens of my phone allows me to look at it critically and determine what is or isn't working. It lets me see if a piece feels to heavy in one area, if there is too much open space and if it feels connected.

I don't rush this process, and I critique my work several times throughout a project this way.

I also like to see the progression of a project from start to finish through pictures!

The same effect was used in blending the top multi-colored fabric with the copper background fabric. The small beads cover the raw edge of the fabric and do not detract from the quilt as a whole.

There are many ways to finish an art quilt and I am not a quilting expert, so I will leave the details to the quilting professionals! In general, I do not like binding, and for this project I felt like an edge with binding would detract from the overall finish. Therefore, I painted the edges with a copper-colored acrylic paint, which stops any fraying and completes the quilt.

Ombré colored tassels added to the bottom as well as purple vinyl tabs added to the top, make this Secret Garden worthy of hanging on any wall that needs a touch of the bejeweled outdoors!

A. 126-2

Explore Further Outside of the Hoop with Embroidery on Paper

Embroidering on paper is both exactly the same as, and yet is completely different from, embroidering on fabric!

What makes it exactly the same? Nothing at all changes about the embroidery. The stitches are all worked in the same way, whether you are stitching on fabric or paper. Even the threads are generally the same. Whether you can use a thicker thread is determined by the weight of your paper. A thicker paper will allow you to use thicker threads. Thicker threads on a thinner paper may weigh it down and make it buckle. The same general rule goes for beads and sequins: match the weight of your embellishments to the weight of your paper.

What makes it completely different? The ease with which you can work through a project changes when you use paper. Embroidering on paper requires a delicacy that is different from embroidering on fabric. Precision in placing stitches matters, because once a needle hole is in paper, it doesn't easily go away. With fabric you can tear out all of your stitches and begin again on the same piece of fabric, but you can't do that with paper. Fabric embroidery is portable and doesn't always need a surface, whereas paper embroidery works best if you have a flat surface to work on.

All that being said, paper embroidery is a fun way to switch up your craft and try a different medium while expanding your knowledge of embroidery. It also opens up new ways of displaying the finished product.

This is an inexpensive print of an original piece by French artist Louis Icart, printed on thick matte paper. For less than $20 at the time, I had a large 12" x 16" piece that was exciting to embroider.

I began by adding black sequins to her skirt. Covering an area completely with sequins gave me a little wiggle room for error, as I began experimenting on this paper. The tension that you use as you pull a needle and thread through fabric will change when you are pulling the same needle and thread through paper. Pulling too hard will result in ripping your paper. The stitches must be worked gently and not pulled too tight.

Because the paper was thick, I was able to add a textured thread to the fringe around her shawl. Again, the stitches required a gentle pull through the paper, so as not to tear it.

This is a delicate process but the impact of a finished piece is worth the extra time and effort that you put into a project like this.

If you want to start a paper embroidery piece but don't want to spend a lot of money on trying it out, I suggest looking around your house for pieces to practice on!

Look at magazine covers, seed and flower catalogs and smaller pieces of generally thicker paper, like greeting cards and postcards.

yazzii.com
yazzii.com

Exploring Even Further Outside of the Hoop with Embroidery on Bags

As someone who has a professed love for all things embroidery and beading related, it makes sense that I need a good bag in which to organize all of my projects, threads, beads and tools.

My Yazzii Craft bags are both incredibly useful and really pretty because of the added appliqué and embroidery. I love being able to tote my embroidery supplies around in something that is also embroidered! Nothing shows a love of your craft like applying it to everyday use.

Using the fabric collage method that you learned in Chapter 2, you can appliqué and embroider onto any bag or tote. It may take some creativity however, because you are working on a surface that has curves and flaps and maybe even pockets. Depending on whether or not you want your stitches to be covered up may also take some ingenuity. But I think by this point you are up for a challenge! So, experiment with a bag you already own and see what it takes to embroider on a fabric that isn't contained in a hoop!

CHAPTER FOUR

Exploring Stumpwork

The term stumpwork encompasses any form of raised embroidery technique and is sometimes simply called raised embroidery. There are several methods that can be used to add dimension to your embroidery and we will be focusing on adding wire shapes, adding stuffing to create dimensional elements, and using embroidery to create dimension with the Couching stitch.

Supplies for Stumpwork

There are a few specialty supplies that you will need to add to your embroidery toolbox if you would like to include stumpwork in your embroidery.

Sewing Stiletto and Stuffing

Stuffing comes in a variety of blends of both polyester and natural materials. In a pinch, when I do not have stuffing handy, I will use cotton balls that I have pulled apart to create stuffing. Choose a variety that appeals to you. You will not need a large quantity of this, so a small bag will last you a very long time!

To fill small areas with stuffing, it is helpful to have a sewing stiletto. A sewing stiletto has a pointed end that allows you to hold the tool and push the stuffing into any area that you wish to fill. If you do not have a sewing stiletto, you can improvise with a toothpick or a bamboo skewer.

Wire and Wire cutters

Wire can be easily found at your local craft store. It comes in a variety of sizes and colors. The higher the gauge number, the thinner the wire, so a 20 gauge wire will be thicker than a 24 gauge. I like to have a selection of colors and gauges to choose from for a project, because you will use different gauges for different effects. A 24 gauge wire is helpful for adding a light hold and bendability to a piece of fabric. A 20 gauge wire would be suitable for adding a firmer hold to the border of a wire mesh fabric when you do not want the item to lose its shape.

You will need wire cutters to cut the small lengths of wire used in making shapes. You can find craft pliers with a wire cutter built into the tool.

Awl

An awl is a tool with a sharp pointed end that allows you to create small holes in your fabric. It can be used for several embroidery related needs, including creating eyelets, attaching shank buttons or piercing holes in fabric to attach wire ends of dimensional items.

Okay, let's jump right into all of the dimensions that you can create on fabric using stumpwork techniques!

Vibrant Blooms and Leaves

This fabric is created from the Vibrant Blooms collection by Shannon Newlin.

The simplest way to begin a stumpwork project is to choose one fabric that appeals to you visually and has lots going on in it. I love this one because of the colors, the birds and the variety of leaves throughout the fabric. In fact, the leaves were my stumpwork inspiration for this hoop.

Begin by hooping up a section of fabric that you love. I wanted to be sure as I positioned the fabric in the hoop, that I had several of the birds contained within. Be sure that your favorite elements are included inside your hoop, and take the time to adjust the fabric so that the layout is exactly how you want it. Remember to try different hoop sizes and shapes.

To add dimension, I began by looking for areas where I could add the Couching stitch. Couching is when your stitching thread goes over a separate piece of thread, making a thicker line of stitching. You can see in these couching examples, that the thickness of the thread can vary. By using a thicker thread, you will end up with a line of stitches that have dimension to them.

I used several of the leaf and circle shapes on the fabric to add couching. When placing your foundation thread around a shape, it is helpful to add a few small stitches to keep it in place.

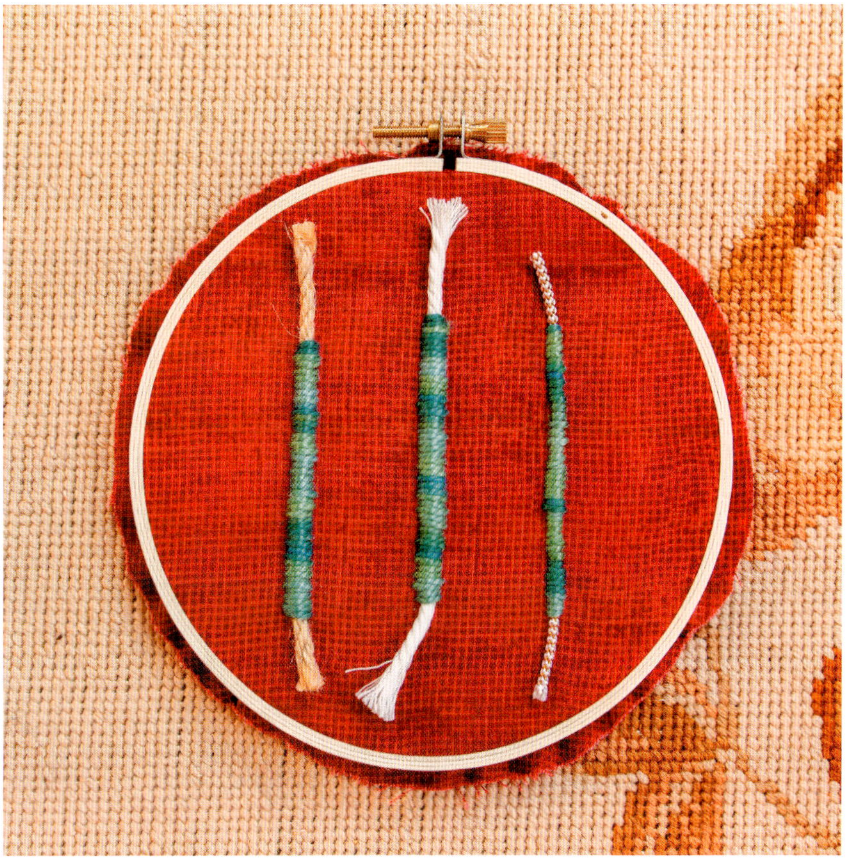

I used some of the remaining non-hooped fabric to create stumpwork leaves that I then added to this hoop. But, before cutting the leaves from the fabric, I used a smaller hoop to place around each leaf and I embroidered it with thread and beads. Then, using the same directions from the box Making Dimensional Shapes, further on, (Page 147), I shaped wire around each leaf and stitched it. After cutting it from the fabric, I used an awl to make a small hole in my hooped-up fabric before inserting the wire ends of the leaves.

The two techniques of couching a thicker thread and adding dimensional shapes, help you to appreciate the individual elements that make up a beautiful fabric. You can experiment with these simple techniques without needing a large stash of fabric to pull from.

A Very Ghastlie Sewing Room

This fabric collage is created from several fabrics from Alexander Henry Fabrics. The collage pieces are layered only on the background fabric and a scene has been created within the hoop. The end result of a collage like this should produce a cohesive feel. As you look at the complete piece, your eye should not focus on any one area. Despite having many pieces, every element should work well with every other. This cohesive look can sometimes be difficult to achieve, but figuring out how to create it is half of the fun, and I will give you some tips to successfully create a scenic collage.

In this piece, the color palette remained minimal. The background fabric is green and the only other colors used are black, white, yellow and pink. Picking from just those colors, I chose one (yellow) to carry it through to every piece. The sewing table is stitched in yellow, the bolt of fabric has yellow details and the dress form has yellow beads scattered throughout. To blend the background with the fabric appliqué, I used the same green colored thread that I had used earlier as I embroidered the lines on each of the background pieces. I also added a simple black Backstitch to tie everything together. Keeping the minimal color palette, allows you to add a lot of detail without confusing the eye.

With this piece, I knew that I wanted to add dimension in the form of stuffed elements, also known as Trapunto. Trapunto is a fun word to say, and it comes from the original Latin word meaning "to prick with a needle." Nowadays, it is simply a quilting technique involving two pieces of fabric. The stuffed element is filled from the backside of the quilt by making a small cut in the fabric and pushing stuffing inside to form a dimensional piece.

However, using this technique on an appliquéd piece is slightly different. Let's focus on her hair. Underneath all of those Bullion Knots, her hair has been stuffed, giving it the appearance of layers and layers of knots. Yet, in reality, it is just one layer of knots on a stuffed surface. When I ironed her in place, I ironed everything except her hair. Because she was ironed in place, it was easy to add a Backstitch outline to her hair, leaving a small section open to add the stuffing. Using a sewing stiletto (you could even use a toothpick), I pushed a small amount of stuffing into the hair until it was full without being overfilled. You don't want your stitches to seem as if they are straining against the stuffing. Once my stuffing was in place, I closed up the small hole with a few Backstitches. Finally, I was able to stitch through the stuffed area to add the Bullion Knots.

When you are adding beads and want them to stand on their own, as I did for the golden scissors, it is best to add them one-by-one, using a small Backstitch or Straight stitch to secure each of them. However, if you want the beads to have a more organically placed feel, as on the bodice portion of the dress form, you can add several to a stitch and then make a smaller stitch so that they bunch up a little. You can also add several to one stitch and make a longer stitch and they will lay flat. Have fun with beads...try stacking different sizes like I did in her boa.

I like to use a variety of buttons when I am working on a stumpwork project. There are two types of buttons that I frequently use: shank and flat.

Shank buttons have the fastener (usually a wire loop) beneath the button. To add a shank button to your work, it is best to use an awl to pierce a small hole in the fabric. Push the wire backing through the small hole and then secure it beneath the fabric with thread. I usually run my threads through other stitches so that they cannot be seen above the fabric. Flat buttons sit flat on the fabric and usually have 2-4 holes. They are simple to secure to the fabric and can just be stitched into place through the holes in the button. Don't limit yourself to buying buttons at craft stores. Antique markets and thrift stores are treasure troves for finding old sewing supplies. One of my favorite purchases was a glass jelly jar filled with old leather and pearl buttons! Always keep your eyes open for once-loved items that you can use in your embroidery.

When you have finished your hoop using the directions found in Chapter 7, you may decide that you want something other than a plain wooden hoop to hold your embroidery. I suggest using acrylic paint or a stain, to drastically change the appearance of your project. Remove the hoop from your finished piece and apply either the acrylic paint or a stain to carefully cover the wood of the hoop. If using paint, it may take more than one coat to fully cover your hoop. If you decide to use a stain, follow the directions and leave the stain on the wood longer for a dark color or for a shorter time to get just a bit of color. A sample size container of stain at the hardware store will last you for ages! Just remember to thoroughly wipe off any remaining stain and let it dry completely before allowing it to touch your fabric.

Branch of Apples

This pattern (Page 210), combines both fabric painting and stumpwork in the form of dimensional leaves and gimp wire (Page 135). Chapter 5 explores fabric painting techniques, so you can refer to that chapter when it is time to paint your branch of apples. You could also use the techniques from Chapter 2 to create a fabric appliqué version of this pattern.

I am always looking for interesting textures and fabrics to add to my embroidery. In this piece, I used small scraps of upholstery fabric to create the dimensional leaves (Chapter 7). Using the techniques in the box Making Dimensional Leaves, I added beads to my wire before stitching the wire to the leaves. I then cut them from the fabric to attach to my project.

Along the branch and the apples, I have added small pieces of gimp, or bullion wire. This is also known as French Wire. It comes tightly coiled in a tube and can be cut to various lengths, stretched out or used as is, to add dimension and visual interest to your embroidery. You can find intricate examples of this wire used in goldwork embroidery, which has its origins in Asia. Goldwork pieces are heavy because of the metal used in the embroidery. They also reflect light beautifully and have an elegant, regal finished appearance. The combination of dimension from the leaves and the bullion wire elevates this simple branch of apples.

Dream Garden Collage

This fabric collage is created with fabrics designed by Amy Reber. It was not created using my typical method of HeatnBond and an iron to adhere the appliqué pieces to the background fabric, as we did in 'A Very Ghastlie Sewing Room' (Page 128). Rather, it was created by cutting out several floral elements from the fabric and then stitching them to the background fabric, with just a few stitches to hold them in place. Once the elements were placed, I stitched the leaves and flowers section-by-section. I then added stuffing to each section before finishing with the embroidery stitches. This method works well if you are not sure which areas you want to add the stuffing to, before you begin your project.

Twisted fabric flowers and macrame leaves made from stranded thread, add to the dreamlike feel of this garden. Mixing in elements from other crafts, like macrame, allows you to creatively repurpose the skills you already possess.

The garden fence embellishment was stitched into place with several stitches and then with vines of Feather stitches and Colonial Knots climbing up and over the fence. The embroidery stitches on this piece came at the end of the project and were meant to fill in areas that had empty spaces. This embroidery takes a backseat to the bold, dimensional flowers and leaves that make up this hoop.

Combining Techniques: Stumpwork and Fabric Painting

In Chapter 5, we will be learning the technique of fabric painting. These next two hoops combine this with stumpwork to create both detail and dimentional texture. Refer to Chapter 5 on Page 148 for fabric painting, when you reach that step in the process.

The Tiger Lily

We live in an old house with an old garden, but only two prior gardeners cared for this tiny patch before us. During our first summer in our house, we were thrilled to find a clump of tiger lilies growing beside our porch steps. Not to be confused with the wild day lilies that thrive in roadside ditches and sometimes go by this name in conversation, real tiger lilies are a bit more crafted, with petals that curve back and show off black freckles that shine like glass. They are usually planted in the back of beds so that their impressive height can show off the flowers above. Isolating just one of these flowers in this project allows us to focus on the raised petals, detailed with the tiger lily's signature black spots.

Whether you are using a round or an oval hoop, begin by placing the fabric in the hoop and tightening it. With a water soluble pencil, sketch the stem of the tiger lily through the center of the fabric. (Pattern on Page 213) Next, draw several leaves attached to the stem. Fill the entire stem with leaves on both sides, even though some will be covered up by the tiger lily flower. I used a dark colored fabric as my background and kept the leaves painted in shades of dark green, because I wanted both to fade into the background once the flower was placed on the fabric. After the paint has dried, you will embroider the leaves. I used the Woven Filling stitch in several green colored threads to stitch the leaves. You want to stitch this before the flower. This is especially important if you are using a woven stitch, because it can be easy for your needle to catch on raised elements, like the flower, if it has been attached before the embroidery is finished. Save the stem stitching until the flower has been attached to the fabric.

I cut the six tiger lily petals from wool felt in order to capture the shape of these from the pattern in the patterns section of this book. You want to use this thicker fabric as it is not see-through and can handle having wire attached to it, without bending under the weight of it. When you have cut the petals, you will next embroider black spots onto them. You can use black seed beads, like I did, or you can stitch Colonial Knots in a glossy black thread. Next you will attach the wire to the underside of the petals. I used 24 gauge wire, which is light enough to be cut easily, to bend to shape with your fingers and to stitch to your petal. Cut a length with your wire cutters, and then stitch it to the petal with a thread that matches the petal's orange color. Continue this process for all of the petals. When each petal has wire attached, stitch the petals down to the center section of the area where you want your flower to be placed. You are only stitching down one end of each petal, so that you finish up with a flower shape once all the petals are in place. Be sure to leave space for attaching the center beaded wires.

Gently fold each petal back so that it creates the raised shape of a tiger lily petal. The wire and fabric can be shaped however you want the petal to look. You can hide your stitches and the end of the petal underneath the front section of it. (This will make sense as you work on each petal of the flower!) Be patient during this process. As you stitch each one, hold your project up so that you can make sure your wire and stitches are not visible as you look at it straight on.

The center wire section of this flower, representing the stamen of the tiger lily, is made with a thicker 20 gauge wire. I used copper colored wire and copper colored size 8 beads. Cut 7-10 small sections of wire, approximately 1¾" long. Bend the end of each piece of wire, creating a closed loop, large enough to hold these seeds in place. Then add the beads to cover a 1" length of the wire. Set aside.

When each section of wire has been beaded, gently twist all of the sections together at their un-beaded ends. Create a loop from this twisted length of wire. Using an awl, poke a hole in your fabric at the center of the flower. Push the looped wire end through and secure it with several stitches on the reverse side of the fabric. It doesn't need to look pretty, it just needs to be secure! After the wire has been attached, you can shape the individual beaded wire sections and reshape the flower petals, which may have shifted around during the securing process. The stem can now be embroidered or beaded. I have used size 8 and size 6 seed beads to stitch along the stem.

Your tiger lily is now finished! You can finish the hoop using the directions found in Chapter 7 and you can decide whether you want to leave the outer hoop on your project or remove it to display.

The Bleeding Heart

Bleeding hearts have a long history in our family. When I was growing up, my mother grew them along the path to our house. I loved when the heart shapes appeared on the plants every year. My husband remembers them peeking from the stone walls that surrounded the patio at his grandmother's house, like trees that hang to the sides of a canyon. Now, we grow them among lady ferns and wild ginger in a shady corner of our garden, under the century-old apple tree. They have delicate flowers that the bees love, popping into full display in early May and disappearing in the blazing heat of July. Like most perennials, we must enjoy them while they last, and if we want them to last longer: preserve them in stitches!

The stumpwork leaves on this hoop were created using DMC's Stitchable Mesh Fabric. If you are unable to find a mesh fabric, you could also create them using a felt fabric.

So, hoop your fabric and begin this project using the Bleeding Heart leaf (pattern on Page 213). Trace or freehand sketch your own layout of stems, leaves and hearts on your hooped fabric with a water soluble pencil. Decide which leaves will be painted on fabric and which ones will be raised leaves made from painted mesh or felt. Paint any leaves and hearts on your fabric and allow to dry.

NEEDLES DOWN!

The Language of Flowers

During the Victorian Era, Floriography, or the language of flowers, was an important language to be versed in. It would have been common during that time, to find a dictionary of flowers and their meanings in most homes. The flowers that made up these small arrangements were just as important as the way the small bouquet, or tussy mussy, was presented to the recipient. If an arrangement was made with flowers that symbolized "love" or "friendship" but was then presented to the recipient upside down, it could mean the opposite of those loving floral sentiments!

There are several floral elements that you can stitch throughout this book. If you wanted to present your loved one with a hoop made of flowers, here are the meanings assigned to the flowers that I stitched. It's important to note that throughout history, several meanings could be associated with every flower, so when making (or stitching) your bouquet, choose your flowers wisely!

Begonia: This is associated with caution and carries a possible warning about misfortunes to come.

Bleeding Heart: The pink heart can symbolize passionate love and romance while the white heart symbolizes purity and innocence.

Crocus: The earliest to arrive in the Spring, these flowers symbolize rebirth and joy.

Dahlias: Another plant that can carry several strong meanings. The flowers symbolize love, inner strength and creativity.

Daisies: These happy flowers symbolize cheerfulness, innocence and new beginnings.

Echinacea: These plants can have healing and medicinal properties. They also symbolically represent strength and healing.

Fern: These leafy plants symbolize fascination and confidence.

Magnolia: This blossom symbolizes femininity and love of nature.

Tiger Lily: Every colored lily represents something different. Orange-colored lilies symbolize confidence and energy.

Tulips: As with lilies, each color represents a different meaning. In general, tulips symbolize love. Yellow tulips can symbolize cheerfulness and hope, while purple tulips carry the meaning of luxury and elegance.

Making Dimensional Shapes

Create your leaves using the steps for creating dimensional shapes. When these are finished, decide how you want to add them to the fabric. You can pierce a small hole with an awl and secure the wire ends below the fabric. In this piece, I simply laid the wire ends on the fabric and attached them with the Couching stitch to the vine. Finish stitching the vines with a stitch that can blend into the stitched wire. I used small Satin stitches and stitched right up to the wire ends so that they could not be seen on the fabric.

Now you can finish embroidering the piece. Add any other embroidered and beaded details to the leaves and hearts on your project. Finish the hoop using the directions found in Chapter 7 and enjoy a bit of the garden inside your house!

Follow the steps below, to create a dimensional shape to add to your embroidery.

Select the shape you want to add dimension to.

Before cutting the shape out of the fabric, embroider any details and add beads or sequins at this point.

When you have finished embroidering, cut a length of wire and bend it to fit the outside of your shape.

Secure it with a few small stitches.

When the wire is secured, add stitching on top of it. Use small Backstitches or a Buttonhole stitch.

Be sure to cover all of the wire with stitches, except for the very ends, where you have twisted them all together.

Carefully cut the shape out of the fabric, making sure you do not cut any of your stitches.

Be patient as this can feel like a tedious step.

I like to have good lighting & make tiny cuts until my shape is removed.

You now have a dimensional shape!

CHAPTER FIVE

Exploring Fabric Painting

Painting a design on fabric that you wish to embroider feels like an awesome accomplishment: the weight of the brush in your hands, the glide of the paint, the lines you imagine and bring into existence.

If the thought of painting something from nothing scares you a little bit, don't worry because I have a great project to get you started in this form of mixed-media embroidery.

Let's talk through the supplies that you'll need before we get into the technique of fabric painting.

When your fabric is at an angle and being held on an embroidery stand, it allows you to see if there are painted areas that light can still shine through.

Sometimes it takes more than one layer of paint to completely fill an area. Holding it at an angle lets you see what parts of your paint need touch-ups.

If you don't have an embroidery stand, try propping your piece at an angle on a stack of books as you paint.

Fabric Painting Supplies

Fabric

The projects that you will see throughout this chapter have been painted on quilting cotton and Aida cloth. Before you begin, it is best to paint a test swatch of your fabric with the paint that you plan on using, especially when you are using colored fabric. Some colored fabrics, especially darker colors like navy, black and evergreen, absorb the paint, altering the paint color that you thought you were using! You may need two or three layers of paint to obtain the actual color that you intend to use.

Embroidery Hoop

For a detailed discussion of embroidery hoops, see Chapter 1 of this book. Because I use hoops throughout the embroidery process, I make sure that my hoop will tighten securely onto the fabric and will not loosen while I work.

Embroidery Stand

As I embroider, I typically hold my project, rather than using an embroidery stand. However, when painting a piece of fabric, I find it incredibly useful to have a stand to hold my piece. I work with the Nurge® Embroidery Table Stand because it is adjustable and can hold my work in multiple positions. It holds the hoop securely and allows adjustment of the angle of my workpiece. This is particularly important when painting on fabric.

Water-Soluble Pencil

Before I paint anything, I first sketch a draft of my idea on my fabric. I use the Clover Water Soluble Pencils. These work well for both drawing freehand and transferring my design from a pattern to fabric, using a lightbox. Since they are water soluble, the pencil marks can be washed off easily with a little water. However, I rarely need to do this, because the paint will flow over them and they will not show up through the paint.

Acrylic Paint

Small bottles of acrylic paint are widely available at craft and fabric stores. I use FolkArt® brand paints, which come in several formulas that work well on fabric, such as Acrylic, Multi-Surface, Metallic, Pearl and Shiny. There are other available formulations, but I would recommend you stay with the ones I just listed. They have always worked well for me, and you can jump right into fabric painting without worrying about mixing your colors and then not having them turn out like you imagined. I think these paints are an excellent choice.

If you would rather mix your own colors, then I suggest you purchase tubes of acrylic paint. My favorite is Arteza® Acrylic Premium Artist Paint. These currently come in a box of 24 tubes. With them, you will have a nice range of colors for use by themselves, or you can mix them and create your own colors.

I like to have a variety of both types of paint, so that when I am working on a project, I can obtain painted results that are exactly how I want them to look.

Fabric Paint Markers

If you want to paint on fabric but don't feel like dealing with all of the accoutrements that go along with painting, then I can highly recommend you use Tulip Rainbow Fabric Paint Markers. These are different from the standard fabric markers, which have their own place in the crafting world. These paint markers will duplicate the effect that you will get when you use paint on your fabric. You can layer colors with these, as there is no bleeding and there are 15 colors that you can work with to create your design. A trial with these might be a great place to start when you want to paint but aren't sure that you are going to be doing it over the long haul!

Brushes

I do not have any specific brands of paint brushes to recommend, because I have a wide variety that I enjoy using. But, I do prefer certain types of brush for fabric painting. I have found that brushes with synthetic bristles hold up better than natural bristles when using acrylic paint. That said, you do not need a lot of brushes to get started. I suggest looking at them in person, if possible, to see what you feel comfortable using. Flat and angled flat brushes are used for putting down initial layers of paint. They are a slightly wider brush, that feels manageable and well under control. You can brush with them flat to fill a wide area with paint, or you can hold them upright and use them to create fine lines. Round and pointed-round brushes are for adding small details or fine lines.

With a few of each type, you are ready to get started using paint on fabric!

Paint Palette

Before starting, you will need something onto which you can pour or squeeze out the paint. This can be anything from a sturdy piece of cardboard, that is just the right size for your work area, to a plastic paint palette or a heavier ceramic palette. I have used all of these options! My favorite is a ceramic palette which is large enough to mix several paint colors in, and is heavy enough not to slide around while I'm dipping in my brush. Start with the cheapest option until you know what will work for your space, and then upgrade as you see fit.

Palette Knife

If you are using tubes of paint and blending your colors, then you will need something to mix them with. A small palette knife works great and will help you to become the next Bob Ross!

Further Reading

Should you want to mix your own paint colors, I have found the book '1500 Color Mixing Recipes for oil, acrylic & watercolor' by William F. Powell to be incredibly useful. Perhaps like me, you are someone who has not had training in color study. This book will give you the basics that you need to know, if you don't want all of your paint mixing experiments to end up brown!

I will be sharing several projects that I created from pictures that I have taken of various botanicals. If this is something that interests you, but you don't have pictures to go by, then the 'Flower Color Guide' by Darroch and Michael Putnam is an excellent resource to look at the color and design of plants.

Painting on a Printed Fabric

Let's get into fabric painting with a project that does not feel daunting. This piece is made with a fabric from the Diving Board collection by Alison Glass. The original fabric is simply blue and white without any other color.

For this project I used the Tulip Rainbow Fabric Paint Markers. If you can color with crayons on paper, then you can absolutely paint with these markers on fabric!

When you are painting on a printed Fabric, I find it helpful to take a photo of the original section that you are painting.

Sometimes, there are detail lines that you paint over and when the paint dries, you cannot see those details anymore.

If your end goal is to go back and embroider the lines and details back into the piece, then it is helpful to have a photo where you can see the original lines.

All of my pieces are painted while in a hoop. The fabric is raised while in a hoop, so there is no worry about paint seeping through the fabric and ending up on your desk. However, it is still a good idea to have your work surface covered whenever you are working with paint.

Before painting, I placed the mermaid section of the fabric in the hoop. I then securely placed the hoop in my embroidery stand so that it was held at an angle. Following the directions on the Fabric Paint Markers, I began with the largest area, the tail of the mermaid, to get a feel for how the paint moved on the fabric. Carefully staying within the lines, I allowed that to dry and then moved on to the smaller flowers and circles around her. It is important not to rub your hand over freshly painted areas as you paint sections of the fabric. This paint does dry fairly quickly and if you want to layer colors over your initial layer of paint, you will not need to wait long.

Before embroidering the finished piece, I waited until the paint felt completely dry and then I added embroidery just like any other (unpainted) project!

Painting without a Pattern

The best way to get writing is to put pen to paper and that same idea goes for fabric painting too: just jump in and put (in this case) water soluble pencil to fabric.

Early on in the COVID-19 pandemic, my family and I, like lots of other people, were taking long walks through the neighborhood. Every day, we passed a beautiful Magnolia tree that was just loaded with flowers. One day, after passing that tree several times, I came home and quickly sketched an abstract version of the Magnolia blossoms onto some fabric.

This was one of my first forays into fabric painting and you will notice the entire design is not painted. I used pink paint to highlight scattered blooms throughout the piece. The other leaves and branches on this fabric were beaded or stitched. I played with the color palette too, focusing just on the shapes of the magnolia blooms. Find something from your everyday life to focus on. Maybe it is winter and you see a tree without its leaves and you like the shape of it. Sketch that! Maybe it is fall and there are leaves scattered on the ground. Pick up a few and sketch those! Play with shapes and lines and experiment with the feel of painting on fabric. Then let it dry and embroider your unique piece of art.

Painting from a Photograph

Living in the suburbs of Philadelphia, also known as America's Garden Capital, we have access to over 30 gardens within 30 miles or so of the city. And that works out to even more botanical inspiration that I can access! But you don't need to visit curated gardens to find inspiration from nature. Any garden or park will have interesting plants and leaves that you can base a fabric painting on. I always have my phone with me and my camera roll is filled with pictures of plants that I like, and close-ups of details that I find inspirational. The following hoops were all sketched by me from photographs that I have taken in my travels. The process for creating each hoop was exactly the same. First, decide on a background fabric and hoop shape and hoop it up. Next grab your photograph and water soluble pencil and draw a few basic lines. Try to imitate the main shapes that you see in the picture. The finer details will come when you are beading and embroidering. Pull out your paints, brushes, palette and a jar of water to clean your brushes. Decide which paint colors match the photograph and put these on your palette.

Start painting! Remember, you may need several coats to achieve the desired look. Allow the paint to dry. Add any painted details at this point. Once you are happy with the results, allow the paint to dry completely, and when it is no longer damp to the touch, you can begin to embroider.

To keep your embroidery in the hoop while removing the outer hoop, you will need to finish it using the directions for finishing a hoop given in Chapter 7. Then simply remove the outer hoop and it is ready to be displayed.

These begonia leaves were painted with just four colors and then were overlaid with embroidery and beads to accent details in the leaves. A border of purple Czech seed beads replaced the hoop border.

NEEDLES DOWN!

Philadelphia: *America's Garden Capital*

Once known as Penn's Woods, Pennsylvania was founded by William Penn and named for the lush woodland forests that once exhisted there. The Philadelphia region is proud of its botanical heritage and has become known as the Garden Capital of America, because of its many public gardens.

Made up of 36 public gardens, found at residences, university grounds and museums. This area has a history of gardening dating back to the early 1700s, when John Bartram began creating a botanical garden along the Schuylkill River in Philadelphia. His interest in nature spurred him to begin an extensive collection of native plants that exists to this day.

The Franklinia tree was discovered in 1765 by John and his brother William, in what is now Georgia and named after their family friend, Ben Franklin. It turns out that this singular grouping of trees must have been among the last, as it is now extinct in the wild. All Franklinia trees growing in cultivation today are direct descendants of the original collection the Bartram brothers brought back to Pennsylvania! Only because the plant is still desirable to gardeners for its unusual bloom time and its smaller habit, does it still exist. Planting a Franklinia is preserving part of the continent's natural history.

Bowman's Hill Wildflower Preserve and Stoneleigh are local gardens which emphasize the importance of native plants, both to benefit the landscape and the pollinators. Using our "Garden Passports" to explore the many gardens in America's Garden Capital, is a favorite pastime for my family.

This echinacea and fern were from a photograph taken in my garden. The combination of these two plants together, is just as beautiful in real life as it is painted in this hoop.

This hoop is an example of adding painted details once your first layer of paint is on the fabric. You will notice in the echinacea petals and the fern fronds, there are several colors layered together to add subtle detail.

Superduo beads enhance the center of the flower with just one hole being secured. This allows the beads to stand up, rather than lie flat on the fabric, so that they imitate the spiky seed head found on the echinacea flower.

I am constantly amazed by the variety of Coleus leaves and am drawn to their nearly neon color palette. I tried to imitate that color palette here with the beads and threads that I chose. The painted fabric leaves take their place in the background, allowing the embroidery to really stand out.

Every year we plant several different types of dahlias in our garden. I say "we" but really my husband does all of the planting and I just do the enjoying! I enjoy the surprise of a different variety of plant that I love so much. To capture that joy, I take lots of photographs and I can't resist recreating my favorite flowers on fabric.

In this hoop, rather than stitching the seed beads with the hole to the side, I stitched each bead with the hole facing up. It is more time consuming to stitch a bead this way, because each has to be secured with four stitches, but the end result gives a unique view of the bead.

NEEDLES DOWN!

The Camera's Eye

Have you ever taken a picture with your phone or a camera and the image looks different from when you saw it with your own eye?

Both the human eye and a camera have lenses to see an object. You can see and focus on an object with the lens of your eye, and your camera can do the same thing. The difference is that when you look at something, the lens in your eye can move the object into focus. Also, it can change shape based on what you are looking at, whether it is moving and the distance it is from you. Your brain also plays a part in what is being seen and focused on.

Your camera doesn't have a brain, so when you point a camera at something, it has several lenses that are designed to capture the shape of what is being seen through the lens. You may even see professional photographers who work with several lenses to capture and render the various images that we can do with our eyes.

When you finish creating a piece of art, whether it is embroidery, a drawing or a painting, photographing it is an important step in the process. Whether you are building a portfolio of your finished pieces or simply taking a picture of a finished piece to share on social media, there are several tricks to photographing a piece of work to capture it at its best.

Photographing your art in natural light will get you the closest color results to what your piece actually looks like. Do not try to take a picture of your piece in full sun as the colors will look washed out. Should you take the picture in early morning light, your piece may have a bluish appearance that you cannot see until you look at it. A picture taken on a cloudy day, in natural light, you will get the best results.

If you have a lot of texture in your piece, beads, textured threads, etc., lighting your piece from the side can help you to capture that dimension in a photograph. Become familiar with editing software. Despite all of your best intentions, sometimes you will need to edit your photos. If you are taking the majority of pictures on your phone, experiment with editing apps until you find something that feels easy and comfortable to work with. I find myself using Adobe Lightroom on my phone for little tweaks to coloring and lighting.

The main takeaway is to be yourself and create your own style. If you are sharing content on social media, have your own photographic style. Maybe that style is sharing only closeups or creating flat-lays with objects related to your art. Have fun and don't be afraid to experiment with photography to capture your personal style!

Painting with a Pattern

If you don't feel comfortable sketching directly onto fabric without creating a pattern first, then sketch out your ideas on paper. This may allow you to feel more relaxed and able to make and erase mistakes or change your mind before putting it on fabric.

Follow the directions given in Chapter 7 where I describe how to transfer a pattern. You will begin with a paper pattern that you then transfer to the fabric.

I have created two patterns; one for a row of tulips (Page 211) and one for a few white daisies (Page 212). These will allow you to try out this method before creating your own pieces from photographs. Both are designed to fit inside of a 9" oval hoop. Like all of my patterns, you can be creative and trace the entire pattern onto your fabric, or you can take a portion of the pattern to make it fit the hoop you would like to use.

This pattern of crocus flowers can be transferred to cotton fabric, just as you did with the previous examples. Alternatively, you can try painting on Aida cloth.

Aida cloth is meant to be used for counted cross stitch. However, I think it is fun to use it unexpectedly in embroidery and combine the finished project with cross-stitch embroidery and free-form embroidery with beads.

Ultimately, painting on fabric gives you the freedom to not just embellish, but design from scratch. It allows you to take your eyes out into the world and bring back the images they capture and make something truly one-of-a-kind. There is some of the wonder of childhood in that process. I hope you will give it a try.

CHAPTER SIX

Exploring Needle Felting

Needle felting can add an entirely different texture into your embroidery pieces and is the perfect craft for people who love fiber.

When you needle felt, you are using a special barbed needle together with loose wool fibers. By stabbing the fibers repeatedly, you will create a matted shape. The barbs on the needle roughen the fibers and help the shape to take on dimension, usually in the form of a sphere or cylinder.

Needle felting can be done directly on fabric to fill in an area or it can be used to create dimensional shapes that can then be added to an embroidery project. There are so many ways to incorporate needle felting into embroidery and in this Chapter we will touch on a few methods.

Needle Felting Supplies

With just a few simple items, you can quickly begin your journey into needle felting.

Felting Mat

As you look for a felting mat, you will see two main types; namely, wool pads and brush mats. I have used both for the felting projects in this book and I definitely recommend using a wool pad. Like needles and scissors, I feel that felting mats are very personal and so you can decide what you like to work with best. Try one of each and see if you get slightly different results by using one type over another.

Wool pads are made of densely felted wool. They are used as the surface for your felting projects. When using one, I put my fabric in a hoop and then set it on the wool pad as I begin to felt my fibers. A mat helps to create resistance with the fibers and it is the motion of the needle punching the fibers that rearranges them, and helps them to take on the shape that you are creating.

A brush mat can be useful for creating dimensional shapes. To create the holly berries you will see later on, I used a brush mat rather than a wool pad. For felting on fabric, I feel that the wool pad offers slightly more resistance, allowing you to felt more easily. However, you can also place a piece of felt on top of the bristles and then felt on top of that to gain more resistance as you work.

Felting Needles

The needles that you use for felting are much different from the ones you use for embroidery. To begin with, there is no reason to thread anything through a felting needle, so there is not an eye in it. Looking closely at a felting needle, you will see that there are barbs on the end. These are meant to catch the fibers as you stab the needle into the fabric. They help to move the fibers so that they make new bonds and enable them to get closer together, gradually eliminating the air spaces, which makes for denser material. Felting needles come in a range of sizes and remember, as with sewing needles, the higher the number, the thinner is the needle. So, a 32 gauge needle is the thickest and a 42 gauge is the thinnest. You will obtain different results from each size in between. I like to begin my project with a 38 gauge needle and then as I'm finishing my project, I will switch to a 40 gauge for the finer details. You will also see a variety of needle felting shapes: triangle, star, spiral/twist and reverse. I find that I get about the same results with the triangle, star and spiral/twist shapes, so choose from among these to get started and see what you like to work with. A reverse needle is for pulling fibers up through your top layer. Thus, if I wanted to felt an object and I have brown as my base layer with red on top, I can use a reverse needle to bring some of the brown fibers up through the red layer.

Fiber

Needle felting is done with a type of material called roving. In the process of going from wool to yarn, roving is the step reached just before it becomes yarn. Roving is much fluffier than yarn and it has already gone through the processes of shearing from the sheep, cleaning it, carding it and dyeing it. When you buy wool roving, you will have a fluffy little ball of fibers that are perfect for needle felting. Roving can come from an animal such as the sheep or from an alpaca; or it can be plant based and made from bamboo, hemp or other fibers. I like to use merino wool roving because the fibers are the right coarseness to felt into the fabric. There are softer fibers that you can experiment with, but they may take longer to felt. Because I love fibers, I am willing to experiment with a variety of them, to achieve a softer or a finer or even shinier result. If you aren't into experimenting and just want a wool roving that will work for all of the projects in this book, then you can't go wrong with merino wool! You will also find you do not need great quantities to finish a project. I recommend the Etsy shop Mohair & More, where you can find 1oz balls of roving in a gorgeous array of colors. A purchase of 1 oz may not sound like a lot, but you will have all that you need and more, with that amount of fiber.

Needle Felting on Printed Fabric

As with most of the techniques throughout this book, I suggest starting with a simple project, using just one piece of fabric. This project does not need to fit within a large hoop, in fact, my favorite starting size is a 6" hoop. Six inches feels substantial enough as you are holding it and adjusting it on the felting mat as you learn to felt. It is small enough so that it doesn't feel like you have taken on a big project that will get set aside in your pile of incomplete projects!

For my project, I have chosen fabric by Tina Givens. The original fabric design has detailed lines throughout the flowers and leaves. When you begin felting, you are covering up all of those lines. Eventually, you will need to make a decision on whether to leave the original lines out of your finished project or whether you will find a way to add them back in. I begin every project like this by using my phone to take a picture of the original fabric. Having the picture of the pre-felting stage is important. Because, as I fill my hoop with wool, I will no longer be able to see the lines. With the picture, we can all look back as we are embroidering details and adding beads, and can replicate what was originally on the fabric.

Alternatively, you could take a piece of fabric like this and felt small areas while leaving others bare. I used this method on the yellow leaf. There were divided sections on the original fabric and I alternated between felting and leaving the fabric visible and embellishing that with beads. Using several techniques adds visual impact to your final project.

In this piece, besides the hair, I chose to felt parts of the flower but then that was it. I also added layers of sequins and beads and the end result is a hoop that seems to be just one piece of fabric rather than the several pieces that it began as.

Needle Felting on Fabric Collage

So you have explored needle felting on one piece of fabric and you are now ready to take your skills to the next level? It's time to up the ante by felting a fabric collage!

The technique for felting on a collage with several layers of fabric versus felting on just one piece of fabric is not any different. However, it can take a bit more time and patience to felt a hoop with several layers of fabric. This square hoop is a mash-up of my favorite Tula Pink and Anna Maria Horner fabrics. Create a fabric collage using the techniques from Chapter 2. My collage begins with a background fabric and then has four layered pieces which are appliquéd to make up the collage. The hair, which I felted first, has a total of three layers: the background, the flower and the hair. As you are creating your collage, think about what you will be felting and how many layers your needle will need to go through. The more layers that you have, the longer it will take you to felt your piece because you are not only going through fabric, you are also going through the adhesive on the back of the fabric. A collage piece like this gives you a lot of choices for what you want to felt. You do not need to felt every single piece of fabric and, in fact, when you pick and choose your areas to felt, the felting blends in with the embroidery, beads, and any other embellishments that you add. It creates a cohesive piece of art where no one method stands out more than another.

Needle felting a collage is a project that will give you immense satisfaction when you finish it, especially if you are able to mix several of the techniques you have learned up to this point.

NEEDLES DOWN!

Unwind and let your hair down!

If you enjoy embroidering with beads and sequins and buttons and embellishments but struggle to hold the weight of the embroidery hoop as you add these trimmings, then you can begin to imagine how heavy the hair of an Elizabethan woman must have been.

During the 16th century, the stylistic choices of Queen Elizabeth influenced the hair styles of many women. Grown very long, hairstyles were then swept up and adorned with flowers. Philip Stubbes, a critic of women's hair and almost everything else during the Elizabethan time, referred to women swathing their hair in "great wreathes of gold and silver" and adorning their hair with "bugles, ouches (jewels or ornaments), rings, gold, silver, glass, & such other gewgaws (baubles) and trinkets." I think it is safe to say that he was clearly not a fan of ornamented hairstyles!

Someone might have read Stubbes criticisms and simply reacted by saying that he needed to just relax and "let his hair down," an idiom that dates back to the 1600s and refers to behaving in an uninhibited manner. It is thought that this literally referred to women and their feathered and flowered hairstyles. When they "let their hair down," it was generally in the comfort of their own private quarters, away from the public eye.

This phrase carried through to the 1920s as women cut their long hair into bobs and both literally and figuratively "let their hair down," embracing the playful freedom that came with shorter hair.

Needle Felting Inspired by Nature

One of the most beautiful things that we took away from various pandemic lockdowns was the forced slowing down of our previously hectic pace of life. We ventured out into nature more often, as so many others found themselves doing. Slowing down allowed us to really look around, taking in small details that might have formerly escaped our notice. This needle felting project is inspired by that time of slowing down and noticing. Whether we were on sidewalk strolls or rambles through the woods, we noticed mushrooms appearing everywhere after days of rain and humidity, and in such variety that no two seemed alike. I gathered pictures on my phone just so I could appreciate the little details later: smooth tops, delicate edges, variations in color. They were all there.

This project is perfect for beginners, because it allows one to experience the delight of needle felting simple shapes. You can use this pattern (Page 214-215) exactly as it is, or you can tailor it to your locale. You may vary your colors and shapes based upon the mushrooms you find locally.

Needle Felting Portraits

These fabric art panels were both created by Melissa Averinos. The gal with the purple hair was created exclusively for use in connection with this book (thank you, Melissa!)

Hair is so much fun to create with needle felting. And it is especially fun when that hair is a funky color and you can play with mixing your colors! So, let's talk about the ways that you can blend colors when working with wool roving.

This piece was created by needle felting individual colors right alongside and on top of each other. There is a mix of reds, oranges, pinks and purples and they were felted with small bits of wool. The result produced by using this method, allows you to see individual colors in the finished piece. To do this, I simply pulled a short length of fiber from one color, needle felted it to the fabric and then added a second color next to that. I continued with this process until her hair was completely covered. When I had finished this, I used a golden yellow roving and added it on top of all of the other colors to achieve a blended look among the variously colored wools.

When you are felting, you can make the decision to felt something until the fibers are so densely woven together that it becomes a dimensional object (see the holly leaves in the project further along in this Chapter) or you can felt them so that the fibers are still visible and it has a fluffier appearance. For the hair in both of these hoops, I loosely felted them so that they are slightly felted but still have the appearance and texture of hair.

Try It! Blending Two Techniques: *Needle Felting & Fabric Appliqué*

I created this multi-technique hoop using the Peach Branch pattern that you will find in the back of the book. Continuing with my series of botanical pieces, the intent here is to blend several techniques. You will notice that the peaches and a few leaves are created with the fabric appliqué technique, while the remaining leaves are needle felted.

Let's make a branch of peaches!

You will begin this project by transferring the entire pattern (Pages 216-218) to your chosen fabric. Using a lightbox (or window), the fabric can be placed on the pattern right side up. Focus on transferring the branch and the leaves that are needle felted completely. The peaches can be lightly drawn in place but do not need to be exact. Because the peaches are made using the fabric appliqué technique and they need to be transferred onto HeatnBond first, there is also a pattern that includes just the peaches in a reversed direction. For this particular project, be sure to transfer the peaches onto the HeatnBond from the pattern that only includes the peaches. If you decide to use this pattern solely as a needle felting or fabric painting project, then simply use the full peach branch pattern. Using the directions for fabric appliqué, choose your fabrics and create your peach pieces from the fabric together with HeatnBond. They can now be ironed into place on your peach branch.

Before beginning the needle felting process, embroider your peaches. I kept my stitches simple on the peach. I used size 8 beads throughout this project and worked the Stem stitch on the peaches and the Feather stitch on the leaves.

Once the fabric appliqué peaches have been stitched into place, you can needle felt the leaves and the branches. This is a good project for you to work on blending several colors of wool roving together. I used three brown colors and three green colors and played around with combinations of these as I needle felted. When the needle felting is complete, you can add any remaining embroidery. I embroidered directly over the felted branch with the Feather stitch and I embroidered along the sides of each leaf with Colonial Knots.

You do not need to use the same combination of stitches or beads that I used. Make this project your own and have fun as you blend the techniques of needle felting and fabric appliqué!

Try It! Blending Two Techniques: *Needle Felting & Fabric Painting*

The Holly branch pattern is an excellent winter project. If you live in an area where color seems to hibernate once fall has ended and before spring begins, you may notice pops of color standing out even more against the many shades of brown outdoors. I have grown in my appreciation of the smallest bits of color during the winter months, much like birds will find the tiniest of berries that remain on native bushes. The holly bush is a prime example of how much joy small amounts of color can bring to a gray day.

Using the holly leaf pattern (Page 215), you can trace several leaves on your fabric. You will notice that I have used an oval hoop and while I was working on my project, I kept the outer hoop on as well. Scatter the leaves on your fabric and then using the techniques of painting on fabric from Chapters 5 and 7, paint on your leaves. Once the paint is dry, it is time to needle felt. My needle felted leaves have a lot of dimension because, rather than felting them directly on the fabric, I traced the leaf pattern onto scraps of green felt and then I felted the felt!

Needle felting on a piece of felt fabric is no different from felting on a piece of cotton fabric. You will have the benefit of varied shades of green, because the felt fabric part of the leaf will be partly visible once your felting is complete. The result is that the leaves can have multiple shades. You can vary your felt fabric and use wool felt or even sheets of craft felt that are available in craft stores. Once your dimensional leaves have been felted, then they can be stitched to the fabric. I added some beads while I was stitching, and they can also be stitched with a green thread. I then embroidered the painted leaves on the fabric. Some I left bare and some are completely beaded. This is a great opportunity to try out some fill stitches or a decorative stitch.

The final step was needle felting the red berries. To create a round object, like a berry, you will start by rolling a small amount of wool like a ball in your hands. Picture yourself as a child, rolling a ball of clay, and that is how you will start a berry. Once you have the round shape, you can felt it just as you would a flat object, while moving it around to keep the circular shape. Add more wool as you go until it becomes a firm shape, rather than a fluffy ball of wool. When you are satisfied with your berry shape, stitch it directly to the fabric. Finish your hoop using the directions in Chapter 7 and if you decide to remove the outer hoop, wait until the fabric has been secured to the inner hoop. Then carefully remove it and display to give yourself some winter color.

Try It! Blending Three Techniques: *Needle Felting, Stumpwork & Fabric Appliqué*

Sunflowers spark joy and now you can create your own floral burst of happiness by using the techniques of needle felting, stumpwork and appliqué. If needle felting intricate shapes feels intimidating to you, then this is a great project to begin with because you will be felting a circular area within a hoop. Using a 5" hoop and a brown-colored background fabric, you will be mixing and matching darker shades of wool roving to create the center of a sunflower. If you look very closely at a sunflower center, you will notice various shades of brown and even some yellow and green mixed in.

Begin with the center section of the hoop and work your way towards the outside. Vary the shades of brown that you use to create a realistic looking sunflower center. Once you have felted the entire circle within the hoop, you can focus on the embroidery. I used Colonial Knots in a thick black thread to mimic the seeds that you would see on the sunflower. There are two layers of petals on this sunflower. The outer petals are larger and created with felt using the largest petal pattern (Page 218). Cut out 8 petals in shades of yellow felt. To give them rigidity, I used the Couching stitch to secure pieces of 20 gauge craft wire on the top of the felt shape. The smaller petals are also cut with felt using the medium sized petal pattern, again as shown on Page 220. Using the pattern for the smallest of the petals, choose a fabric that will become the top layer and follow the directions for fabric collage in Chapter 2. Adhere the smallest petal to the medium sized petal. Each petal can then be added to the hoop by attaching the bottom of the petal to the fabric. You can simply stitch the petals flat to the fabric or you can give them a small fold at the bottom and then attach them that way. The hoop can remain on the project because the petals will cover it up. Using the hardware at the top, the hoop will also double as a way to suspend your piece. Hang this on a wall or even use it as a wreath on your door to welcome Summer and Fall!

CHAPTER SEVEN

Exploring Techniques

This Color Wheel pattern (Pages 219-220), is sized to fit within an 8" embroidery hoop while the stumpwork hoop is 9". Four of the techniques are shown inside an 8" hoop: fabric collage, beading and embellishing, fabric painting and needle felting. My pattern will fit from edge-to-edge within the 8" hoop. You can resize it if you would like it to fit an even smaller hoop. Or, you can use the pattern as is and place it in a 9" hoop so that you have a small border of fabric or have room to upsize the pattern.

When you have made a copy of this pattern, it is best to decide on your color palette before doing anything else. Print an extra copy of the pattern and fill it with the colors you would like to see together. It doesn't need to be pretty, this is purely functional. Doing this first will give you the visual that you need to decide if your palette works for you or not. Later it will help you as you gather your fabrics, beads, paints and wool for the various techniques. As you work through these techniques using this pattern, you have several options. You can ignore the border lines completely and have the beads or the wool blend sit side-by-side in each section. Or you can wait to stitch the borders after you have finished with the technique you have chosen. If you are beading this hoop, you can add the beads for each border first and then fill in the areas with color. How you proceed to work through these decisions is up to you and everyone will choose to work through this project in a different way. Learning the basic techniques for each method will help you along the way!

Technique: Fabric Appliqué

Begin by gathering the supplies to transfer the pattern and create the hoop. You will need a background fabric, fabrics to create each appliqué piece of the color wheel, an embroidery hoop, a light source (window or lightbox), a copy of the pattern, HeatnBond Lite, glue stick and something to write with. For more information on all of the supplies needed, refer to Chapter 2: Exploring Fabric Collage.

Prepare the background fabric by ironing it and placing it in the hoop. Leave approximately 2" of fabric around the edges of the hoop. You will be removing this fabric from the hoop before ironing any other pieces on, but this extra two-inch margin will ensure that you cut the right amount of fabric for the background.

Using the paper pattern, decide on the fabric placement for the colors on the color wheel. Cut a small swatch of each fabric and glue the swatch onto the paper pattern to serve as a guide. You can also number each piece of the color wheel pattern. Creating fabric swatches and numbering the pattern is an optional step, but I find it helps to keep this process organized.

So now we need to transfer the pattern onto a piece of HeatnBond. Place the paper pattern on the light source, reverse side up. (This is a rule of thumb for all fabric appliqué that comes from a pattern: whenever transferring it to HeatnBond, you always want to reverse the pattern, tracing it wrong side up.) Trace the pattern onto the HeatnBond. Copy any directions, such as where the top and bottom of the pattern fall and the piece numbers, onto the HeatnBond and then cut out the large circle of the color wheel pattern.

This large circle you just cut out will serve as the guide for arranging each piece on your background fabric. I recommend cutting the HeatnBond pattern apart, piece by piece, as you go. This is a slow process that takes time, but when you need a pattern to fit back together like a puzzle, these extra steps make sure that everything fits together nicely in the end.

Cut one piece from the pattern and iron it to the reverse side of the colored fabric that you have chosen to appliqué. Once the HeatnBond has adhered, cut this piece out of your colored fabric. You now have your first completed pattern piece. It will have a paper backing and the fabric will be right side up. Peel the paper backing from the fabric, as if you are peeling off a sticker, and you will see the shiny side of the pattern piece.

To get the correct placement on the background fabric, use the large circle of the HeatnBond pattern as a guide. Place it centered on the background fabric with the shiny side up. You have just cut one piece from this and you can place that fabric piece back in the spot where it belongs. This is where it feels like you are putting a puzzle back together. You can choose to iron the piece in place now, or you can wait until you have followed this process for each of the remaining pieces.

Continue until the pattern has been assembled from the fabric pieces.

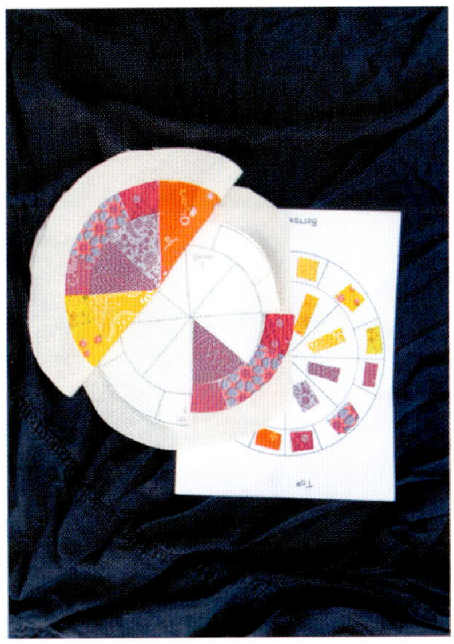

When each piece has been ironed into place, you are ready to place the fabric in the hoop and begin to embroider your project!

Transferring a Pattern to Fabric

The technique of fabric appliqué is the only method where you will first transfer the pattern to HeatnBond. For all of the remaining techniques, you will transfer the pattern directly to the fabric. The same supplies and transfer methods will work for beading, painting, stumpwork and needle felting.

Begin by gathering the supplies needed to transfer the pattern to the fabric. You will need a light source (window or lightbox), a copy of the pattern, a piece of fabric that is approximately 2" larger than the hoop you will be using and a transfer pen or pencil.

I use Clover Water Soluble Pencils to make marks and transfer patterns onto fabric. These marks can be washed away with water.

Tape the pattern in place (right side up) so that it doesn't shift around. Place the fabric on the pattern and trace the pattern onto the fabric with a transfer pen or pencil.

Place your fabric in the hoop, centering it and gently pulling the fabric taut. Tighten the hoop. Trim the fabric, leaving approximately a 2" excess, all the way around the hoop.

Proceed to the directions for the technique that you will be using.

Technique: *Beading & Embellishing*

Gather the supplies you will need for your project: a variety of beads, sequins and buttons in the colors you have chosen for your wheel. You will also require a needle and thread. Refer to Chapter 1: Exploring Embroidery, for a list of embroidery supplies and suggested threads.

With your fabric in the hoop and prepared with the pattern, begin by choosing the largest beads for your project. Stitch several large beads onto each section, using the colors you have determined for your pattern. If you are using sequins or buttons, these should also be stitched down at this time, to make a base layer for your beads. At this point, if you are also beading the borders, you should choose the bead colors you would like to use. Stitch the beads to the borders using a Backstitch, Stem stitch or Straight stitch. Once your borders have been stitched (if you are beading them) and your large beads are stitched down, it is time to add the rest of the beads to the project. Stitch the beads into each section from largest to smallest. In this way, you will be sure to accommodate all of your large beads and

then the small beads can help you to fill in any gaps. Keep in mind that larger beads need to be stitched to the fabric multiple times to keep them in place. I will stitch the bead in place once, and then create a new stitch to go through the hole one more time to make sure it is really secure. This is a simple process but it may be the most time-consuming technique from this section! Make sure you can sit somewhere that is comfortable, grab a drink and snack and have a surface to rest your hoop on as it becomes heavier from the weight of the beads.

Refer to the section on finishing your hoop when you have completed beading your fabric.

Technique: *Fabric Painting*

Begin by gathering the supplies that you need: a paint palette, paints, brushes and your pattern transferred to fabric. For more details on all of the supplies that you will need, refer to Chapter 5: Exploring Fabric Painting.

Taking it section-by-section, you will begin to paint the fabric. Remember it can be helpful to first test your brush and paint on a separate piece of the fabric. Notice how well the paint covers up your pattern markings. If you are using a darker paint, you may be fine just painting over the lines once. But a lighter paint may not cover them up, so you will need to remove them before you begin painting a section. Let one layer of paint dry before adding a second layer. Examine it from several directions to be sure that all areas of the fabric are covered. Sometimes the fabric will absorb the paint differently on printed versus plain fabric, and so it is important to always give it one final look to ensure you have complete coverage. Let the paint and fabric dry completely before adding any embroidery.

Technique: *Stumpwork*

Gather all of the supplies you will need to create the stumpwork version of this color wheel pattern: a variety of colored felt, stuffing, an awl or sewing stiletto and a glue stick.

Two things are essential at the start of this project if you're to get it right.

First, number each piece of the paper pattern before cutting it at all. This keeps you organized and prevents confusion.

Second, use the transfer method described earlier in this chapter to trace the center portion of the color wheel pattern onto your base fabric. Then center the base fabric in a hoop, pull it tight and set aside.
Now it's time to pull out your scissors and start cutting into that paper pattern!
Lay each small piece onto the felt or wool of your chosen color palette. As you cut each piece, set it on its corresponding place on your hooped-up base fabric.

After this layout of the pieces of the color wheel is complete, use a few dots of glue on the back of the fabric to secure each piece. I like to use glue on the top edge of the piece so that it does not interfere with the stuffing process.

Once the pieces have been gently glued in place, add a row of stitching on the outside of each. I have stitched a row of Backstitches on my center section and the Feather stitch on the inside line of each piece. You can stitch this section-by-section or you can stitch the entire piece before stuffing.

Flip the hoop over and on the back side of each piece, poke a small hole through with your awl. Make sure that the hole only goes through the background fabric and not through your colored wool or felt. If necessary, you can carefully enlarge the hole with a pair of embroidery scissors.

Using just a small amount of stuffing, and the blunt end of the awl, push some of the stuffing into the hole. With the pointy end of the awl, carefully guide the stuffing into place. You do not need a large amount of stuffing for this process. Be sure that the stuffed area is not so full that it pulls your pattern piece off the hoop. You do not want it to look like the piece is straining to hold itself together!

The hole in the back of your piece does not need to be stitched up when you have finished. It should be small enough so that the stuffing remains inside without any problems.

Repeat this process for each piece, then add any embroidery and beadwork to the front of your color wheel. This process can be repeated for all of the remaining pieces of this pattern. Or, you can simply glue the remaining pieces into place and add embroidery and beading without stuffing them, just as I did in the sample piece above.

Does any of this seem overwhelming? You can find video tutorials for most of the techniques I use on my Nichole Vogelsinger YouTube channel!

Technique: *Needle Felting*

Gather the supplies that you will need to begin needle felting your project: a felting mat, felting needles and wool roving. I like to have both a medium and a fine felting needle to interchange while I am working on a project.

Place your hooped fabric on top of the felting mat. Beginning with the center portion of the pattern and the medium needle, choose a small amount of your first color and follow the outline of the pattern to start filling in the first section. As you punch the needle up and down through the fabric into the felting mat, you will see the wool begin to adhere to the fabric. Continue until the shape is outlined in your chosen color. Keep in mind that as your wool is adhering to the fabric, it is also adhering to the felting mat below your fabric. That is normal, but remember to remove your fabric from the mat every so often so that they do not completely stick together.

Once the section has been outlined in your color, go back over it and fill in with the wool. Alternate between your medium and fine needles. The fine needle is the last needle you will use when the area is completely covered with wool. You are just adding the last bits of color. Repeat this process for every section on your hoop until the entire color wheel has been felted.

Finishing a Hoop

When you have finished your project using any of the techniques from this Chapter, it is time to handle the excess fabric around your hoop so that it looks polished and complete. Begin by tightening the fabric in your hoop. Sometimes when you have been stitching, or beading or needle felting, the fabric loosens and needs to be tightened. Gently pull the fabric taut and tighten the screw on the hoop. Turn the hoop over and trim away the excess fabric so that you are left with approximately 1/4" to 1/2". When you fold the fabric back, you do not want it to be touching the fabric of your hoop.

Along the back edge of the hoop, run a strip of washable school glue all the way around and then fold the fabric over the hoop. Your hands will get a little messy as you bend the fabric over, making sure that it is overlapping the wood of the hoop. Allow the glue to dry and your hoop is complete!

Optionally, you can add a piece of felt to the back of your work so that your stitches are not visible. I prefer to see my work when I flip it over, so I rarely cover it up. But if you want to gift a project with your stitches hidden, the felt can be pressed into place and it will sit there without any additional sewing or gluing. Hang a ribbon from the hardware and you can now add it to a gallery wall or gift it to a friend!

CHAPTER EIGHT

Showcasing The Blossom Motif

We've explored the color wheel pattern in several ways and you are now ready to go off on your own and create! But, before I unleash you to explore your creativity and gather all of your stitching supplies, let's look at one more project that you can try on your own.

The Blossom Motif pattern can be found in the pattern section of this book (Page 221). From the outset I wanted this pattern to be simple enough for a beginner to try, using any of the methods that we have already discussed: fabric appliqué, beadwork, stumpwork, fabric painting, and needle felting. The pattern has simple shapes and curves, yet the finished project looks anything but simple.

The blossom motif was chosen because of my (self-confessed) love for botanical shapes. I have worked the pattern using each of the five methods. I used the same color scheme for each hoop so that you can see how similar yet how different they all look, when you create them using different methods from one pattern.

NEEDLES DOWN!

An Array of Botanical Shapes

As you approach designing your own botanical motifs, it may help you to know that there are approximately eighteen different shapes of flowers (and this number may vary from botanist to botanist!).

Flowers can first be broken down by their symmetry. If you place a line across the center of a flower, are the two sides symmetrical? If they are, then the flower is considered to be radially symmetrical. If the top of the flower is different from the bottom but the sides are similar, then that is considered to be bilaterally symmetrical. The Bleeding Heart flower would be bilaterally symmetrical, while a zinnia flower would be radially symmetrical.

Once the symmetry has been determined, flowers can fall into various classes.

Small flowers with 4 petals that make a cross shape, fall into the cruciform or brassica family. There are over 4,000 types of plants that fall into this species, including vegetables. If you let these vegetables bolt, you will see the 4-petaled flowers on cabbage, turnips, kale and broccoli, to name just a few.

American Bellflowers and Canterbury Bells, with their cup or bell-shaped flowers, are in the campanulate family. There are about 420 different plants that fall into this category and many of them grow in meadows and woodlands.

Stellate flowers are star-shaped, like lilies. These flowers may look as if they have lots of petals making up the star shape, but if you look very closely, you will see that they have both petals and sepals. The petals are the innermost part of the flower that attract pollinators. The sepals are the outermost part of the flower that act as protectors for the inner petals. This combination of petals and sepals can also be referred to as the tepals.

Dandelions, daisies, asters, coneflowers and zinnias all are in the ligulate shaped family, which includes approximately 1,000 types of flowers. Ligulate means "strap-shaped" and flowers with this shape have petals that radiate all the way around from the center. Many flowers with this shape are valued for their showiness.

Fabric Appliqué Blossom Motif

The collaged version of the Blossom Motif was created using the Chalk and Charcoal line of fabrics from Jennifer Sampou for Robert Kaufman Fabrics.

Using the fabric collage method, I kept the stitching to a minimum on this piece. I worked two rows of Backstitch along the edge of each piece and they were then woven together with a contrasting thread to give it a two-toned look. To create this embroidery technique, first stitch a row of Backstitches along the outer edge. Follow this with a second row beside the first row, making sure you have the same number of Backstitches side-by-side. Then, choose a contrasting thread and come up at the bottom of one Backstitch. All of the remaining stitches are worked on top as you weave the thread back and forth between the Backstitched rows, connecting them so they look like one stitch.

You can create your Blossom Motif exactly how I have, or you can add other details. You may like a border around the outside edge of the hoop, or a row of Backstitches around the motif to make it unique to you.

Beaded Blossom Motif

While my earlier collaged Blossom Motif did not have any beadwork, this beaded version is completely blinged out with beads! The difference between the weight of each of these hoops is substantial.

I began by tracing the pattern onto this hoop. Then I went through my selection of beads. Starting with the largest beads in each of the colors, I sewed them to each of their sections so that I could keep track of my color scheme. It also helps to sew the biggest beads and buttons into place first, saving the tiniest ones for last. These can then be nestled into any open spaces that you have left. While this can look like a complicated pattern to create with beads, it is actually a very relaxing process. I enjoy sorting through beads, finding the colors that match, and then stitching them onto the fabric.

The embroidery is not complicated: each bead is held in place with a simple Straight stitch. For the most part you cannot see the beading thread in a project like this, but I still suggest choosing thread colors that match your beads and fabric.

A beaded version of any pattern takes time and patience. It is also the sort of project where I suggest you take photos along the way, so you can map your progress and see any areas that may need additional beading. Looking at a photo of your project can quickly help you to see if an area needs more of one color or less of another. Photos help me to both critique my work and make better decisions as I progress forward.

Painted Blossom Motif

If you are going to be picking your favorite from these hoops, you should know that the painted version was the hands-down winner among my husband and boys, who, by the way, can be very vocal and opinionated when it comes to my work!

I mixed my own colors of paint to match the shared color scheme of these hoops, rather than using ready-made colors. There are also several layers of paint in each section of the motif. I started with the darkest base color and then added lighter colors on top, so that you could see highlights and shadows throughout the finished painted version. When it was completely dry, I added the stitching to the petals first and chose to keep a minimal number of stitches on this piece. Using a variegated thread in seven colors on the petals, I added Lazy Daisies. The variegated thread works well against the paint, which is also a blend of colors. The edge of each petal is stitched in the Stem stitch and I added a size 8 seed bead to each of them. The Trellis stitch (from my previous books) is a great fill stitch for leaves, especially when you are using a variegated thread. I love the combination of paint on the fabric with the thread layered on top of it. This produces a slight shine and is a great mix of subtle textures.

Padded Satin Stitch Stumpwork

Begin by cutting a felt shape to the desired size. Apply a dot of glue to hold the shape in place.

Using a thicker thread (I used DMC Cotton Retors Mat), create a layer of Satin stitches that do not go from edge-to-edge on your felt piece. You need to leave a small border of unstitched felt remaining.

For the next row of Satin stitches, continue using a thicker thread (I used DMC Tapestry Wool) and work the stitches in the opposite direction.

Your finished shape will have a raised appearance and only you will know the secrets that are below the top layer of stitching!

Alternatively, and for a really raised shape, you can stack several pieces of felt with each piece smaller than the last and then add your satin stitches over that pyramid of felt.

Needle Felted Blossom Motif

The needle felted version of this motif is soft and highly textured. I used my own method of color blending to create a variety of colored wool roves, before I began felting. To create the blue section, I mixed five colors together to achieve this moody blue with neon accents. Once I had each section of wool adhered to the fabric, I went back over the piece, section-by-section, adding individual colors to those areas which I felt could use more of a certain color. I worked this section from the center to the outer edges. Working like this means that you won't be constantly resting your working hand on the finished felted wool sections, thereby flattening all of your work.

After needle felting the entire piece, I added simple embroidery to the leaves using the Feather stitch and added a size 8 seed bead to each outstretched line of the stitch. Each bead was moved into the place where I wanted it on the stitch, then the thread was pulled taut before I moved on to the next stitch. This ensured that the bead stayed in place on the wool. Using varied lengths of Straight stitches and size 8 beads in several finishes, added detail to each petal.

And now, my dear stitchers, I think you are more than ready to go out and create your own projects full of beads and fiber and thread and texture and color and fabric. Gather your supplies and Boho your world!

Conclusion

Well, the time has come. It's time for me to pass the needle and thread on to you as you begin, or continue along in, your creative stitchery journey. What should you do next? I'll tell you what I do after taking in lots of information and I need to process it all: Go outside. Just get yourself outside, whether that means sitting in the sun in your backyard for some Vitamin D, taking a walk through your neighborhood, or visiting a nearby park for some relaxation. Mull over your next project. Think about the supplies you want to gather, look for inspiration in flowers and trees, breathe some fresh air, and then get started.

Begin small with one of the patterns or ideas from this book. Use the supplies you already have, especially if that means you will get started on something right away. Don't feel like you have to rush out and buy every supply item that I mentioned. A needle and some fabric and thread will get you started on your journey. Gather beads and embellishments and fibers as you go. Begin with a stitch sampler and just CREATE!

The sense of accomplishment that you will feel after making your first few stitches, and then a few more, and then completing a hoop, does not go away. It just makes you want to create more! I hope you will stay in touch. I want to learn from your variations on these techniques as well. Share your progress with me, @wildboho, on social media and tag me in what you are working on. Follow along with me and I will do the same for you!

It's time to pull those needles out and: Let's get stitching!

NEEDLES DOWN!

Daily Rituals and Creative Quirks

Artists can be quirky creatures. As you create, you may even find that you have some quirks or rituals that distinguish you from other creatives.

Have you ever wondered about the oddities that your favorite artist might have had? Did you know that:

Georgia O'Keefe spent her summers at Ghost Ranch in New Mexico. As well as having a studio within her house, she also had what she called her favorite studio: a mobile one at that. Made from a Model A Ford, she removed the driver's seat and turned the passenger seat backwards. From there, she was able to spend time, safe from the desert bees and scorching summer sun, immersed in the stark desert landscape.

Red Hot Chili Peppers bassist, Flea, kept bees in his spare time. Early on in his hobby, he had an estimated 200,000 bees in the hives in his backyard. Posting pictures of his bees and their honey on social media helped to draw attention to the plight of the declining honeybee population.

Composer Igor Stravinsky found exercise in the morning was essential to his composing. When faced with a creative block, he would do a headstand which he felt cleared his head and relaxed him enough to continue to work.

When not writing, Charles Dickens might be found combing his hair. Believed to have had traits of Obsessive Compulsive Disorder, Dickens was known to comb his hair hundreds of times a day. He was also very particular in the placement of objects in his office and furniture in the bedroom and was fond of cleaning.

Musicians Neil Young and Rod Stewart are model train aficionados and create elaborate layouts when not performing. Neil Young's Lionel O-gauge layout covered 1,000 square feet among his outdoor gardens. His collection was so large and varied that he began working with Lionel trains and became part owner of the company. Rod Stewart's attic layout featured life-like scenery and buildings. He would work on pieces of his layout during his tours, even requesting an additional hotel room so that he could construct various structures.

Both Virginia Woolf and Nichole Vogelsinger wrote while standing up. In Woolfe's case, it was most likely because she was competitive. Her sister, Vanessa Bell, was a painter and painted standing up. Virginia didn't want her writing to seem less important than Vanessa's painting and so she would stand while writing. In Nichole's case, it was because of her need to always be multitasking while writing. Probably not the most efficient use of brain space, but sitting down and concentrating are not synonymous.

RESOURCES and SUPPLIES

Art Prints for Embroidery

Heritage Posters

www.etsy.com/shop/HeritagePosters

Beads

Shop for Czech seed beads and a variety of other beads

www.johnbead.com

Clover Water Soluble Pencils

www.clover-usa.com

Craft Wire

hildie & jo wire

www.JOANN.com

French Bullion Wire The Designers Stop

www.etsy.com/shop/

TheDesignersStop

Embellishments

Browse for a variety of Tim Holtz embellishments

www.timholtz.com

Embroidery Hoops

DMC • Shop for Wood, Square and Triangle Hoops

www.dmc.com

Fabric Sources

Alewives Fabrics, Maine

Shop online for a carefully curated selection of quilting cotton fabrics

www.alewivesfabrics.com

Alison Glass

Shop for the Diving Board collection and other fabrics great for fabric painting

www.alisonglass.com

www.alisonglass.com/diving-board

Alexander Henry Fabrics

Shop for the Ghastlies Fabrics collection and more.

www.ahfabrics.com

Amy Reber

Shop for her latest fabric designs

www.amyreber.com

Anna Maria Horner

Shop for her latest fabric designs as well as needlepoint, fabric and other embroidery notions

www.annamariahorner.com/fabric

Art Panels by Melissa Averinos

Shop for Professor Kitty or both of the needle felted ladies plus additional original artwork

www.yummygoods.com

Hawthorne Supply

Shop online for the newest in quilting cotton fabrics

www.hawthornesupplyco.com

Jennifer Sampou

Shop for the Chalk and Charcoal collection as well as all of her other fabric lines

www.jennifersampou.com

Pennington Quilt Works, New Jersey

Shop in person or online for a constantly updated selection of fabrics. Also a great resource for online and in-person classes!

www.penningtonquilts.com

Tina Givens

Be inspired by her art and fashion

www.tinagivens.com

Tula Pink

View her latest designs and learn which shops carry them

www.tulapink.com

Aida cloth and mesh fabric

www.everythingcrossstitch.com

Fiber Sources

Anchor Crafts

Shop for Stranded Cotton and Tapestry Yarn

www.anchorcrafts.com

DMC

Shop for Tapestry Wool and Cotton Retors Mat

www.dmc.com

Koigu

Shop for KPPPM Needlepoint Yarn

www.koigu.com

Mohair and More
Shop for Wool Roving

www.etsy.com/shop/mohairandmore

Rainbow Gallery

Shop for Rainbow Tweed, Silk Lame Braid, Sparkle Rays, Splendor, Very Velvet

www.rainbowgallery.com

Sue Spargo

Shop for Eleganza Perle Cotton, and Rainbow Gallery Aurora, Petite Very Velvet, Rainbow Tweed, Shepherd's Silk, Silken Pearl, Splendor

www.suespargo.com

The Thread Gatherer

Shop for Aurora, Sheep's Silk, Silk 'N Colors, Silken Pearl, Sparkle

www.threadgatherer.com

Weeks Dye Works

Shop for Pearl Cotton and Stranded Cotton

www.weeksdyeworks.com

Wonderfil Specialty Threads

Shop for Perle Cotton, Dazzle, Fruitti, Tutti

www.shopwonderfil.com

Fiskars Scissors

Titanium Micro-Tip Easy Action Scissors

www.fiskars.com

Iron and Adhesives

Oliso

Mini Project Iron

www.oliso.com

Project Wool

14"x14" Felted Quilting Mat

www.projectwool.com

Thermo Web

HeatnBond Lite Iron-On Adhesive

www.thermoweb

Elmer's

Washable School Glue Sticks

www.elmers.com

www.elmers.com.glue-sticks

Needles

Richard Hemming & Son

www.colonialneedle.com

Needle Felting Supplies

Brush Needle Mat

www.clover-usa.com

Felting Mat
Hand Carders

www.woolbuddy.com

Felting Needles

www.clover-usa.com

www.etsy.com/shop/CupidFalls

Nurge Embroidery Table Stand

www.nurge.net

Paint

FolkArt Acrylic Paint

www.plaidonline.com

Arteza Acrylic Premium Artist Paint

www.arteza.com

Tulip Rainbow Fabric Markers

www.tulipcolor.com

Sewing Stiletto

www.iheartulapink.com

Yazzii Craft Bags

Shop for a variety of hand-made craft bags.

www.yazzii.com

Further Reading

1500 Color Mixing Recipes for oil, acrylic & watercolor
By William F. Powell

Flower Color Guide
By Darroch and Michael Putnam

Boho Embroidery: Modern projects from Traditional Stitches
By Nichole Vogelsinger

Boho Embroidery: The Pattern Collection
By Nichole Vogelsinger

Boho
EMBROIDERY
The pattern
collection

Boho
EMBROIDERY

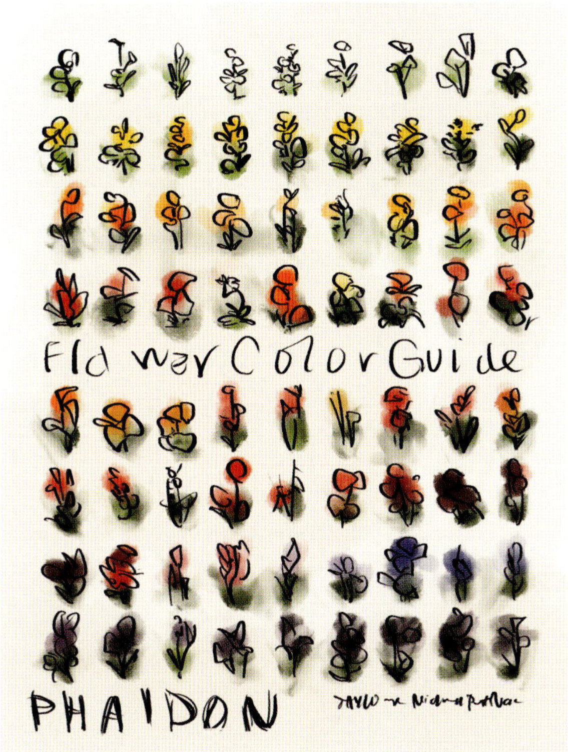
Fld wer Color Guide
PHAIDON

1500
Color Mixing Recipes
for oil, acrylic & watercolor

NEEDLES DOWN!

Further Reading Distractions

Botanical Shapes
www.lizzieharper.co.uk

Collage
The Collage Ideas Book
by Alannah Moore

Creative Quirks
Daily Rituals: How Artists Work
by Mason Currey

Embroidery Slates
www.letempsdebroder.com

Sequins
www.smithsonianmag.com

Victorian Hair
www.hairarchives.com
www.elizabethancostume.net

The Little Hands
www.hautehistory.co.uk

Pattern for Stitch Samplers on Pages 50-59

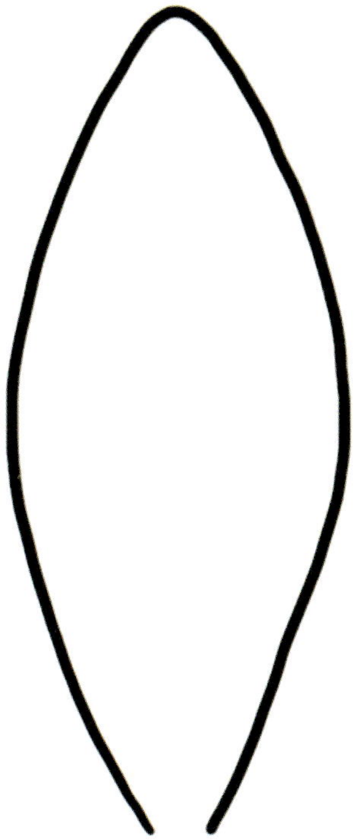

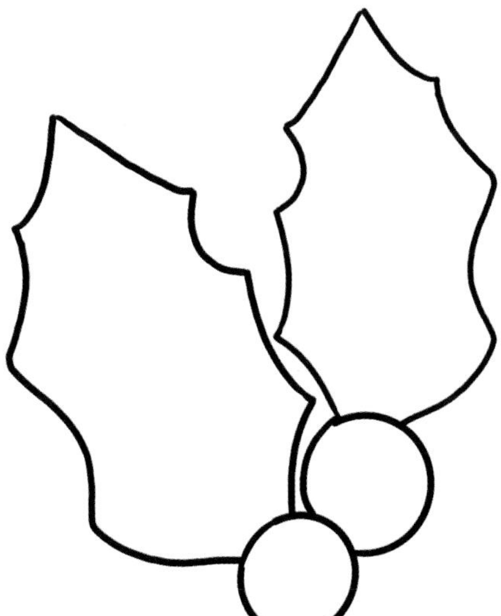

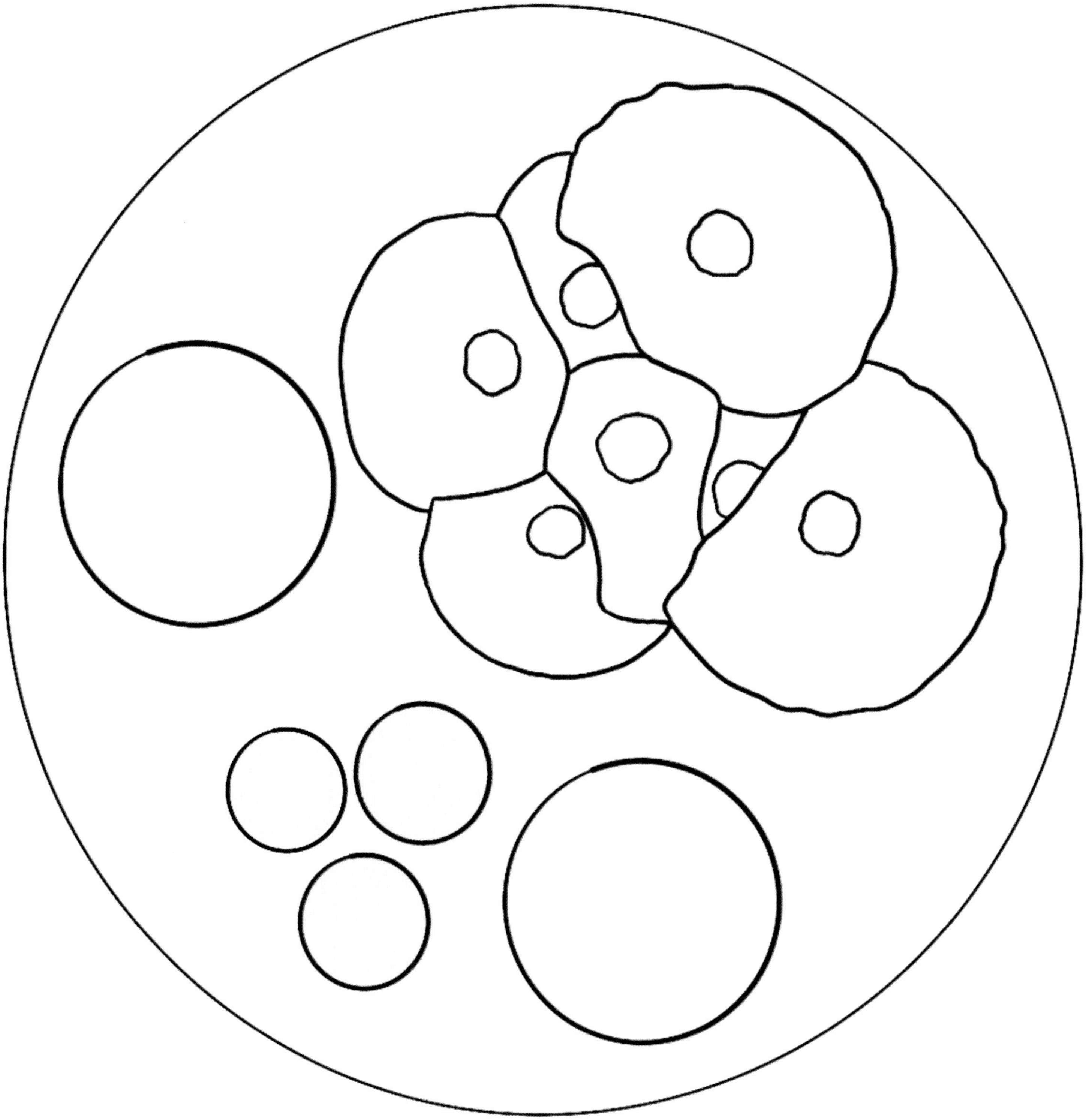

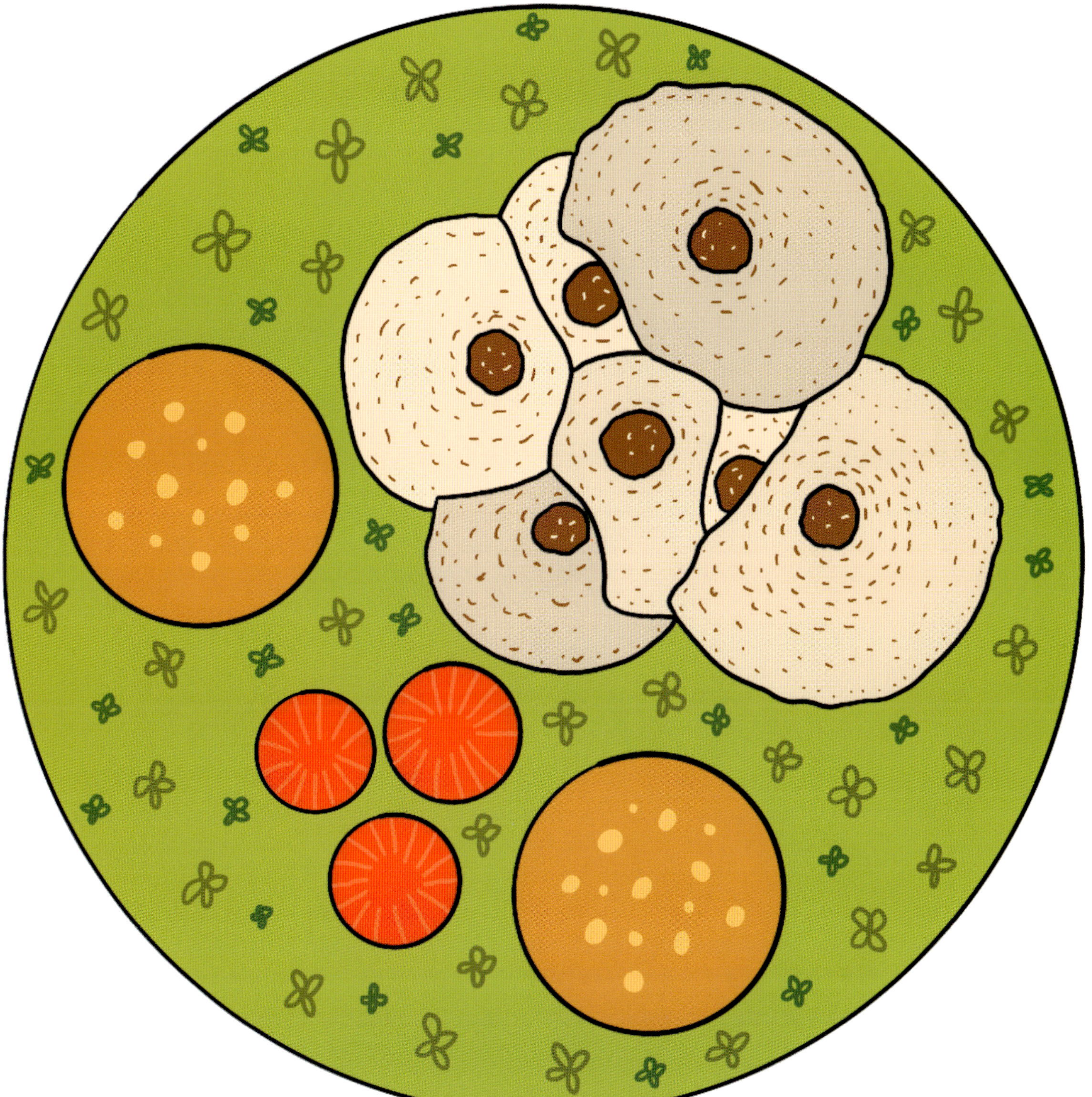

The Patterns

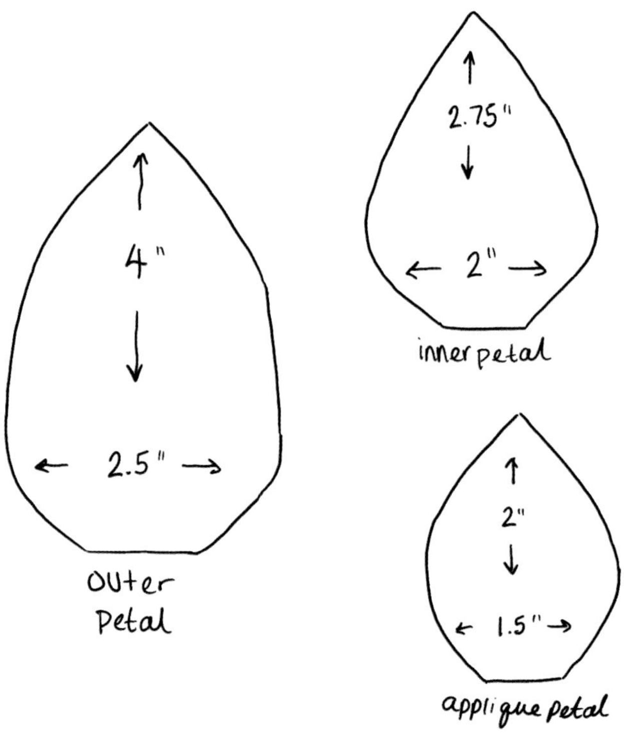

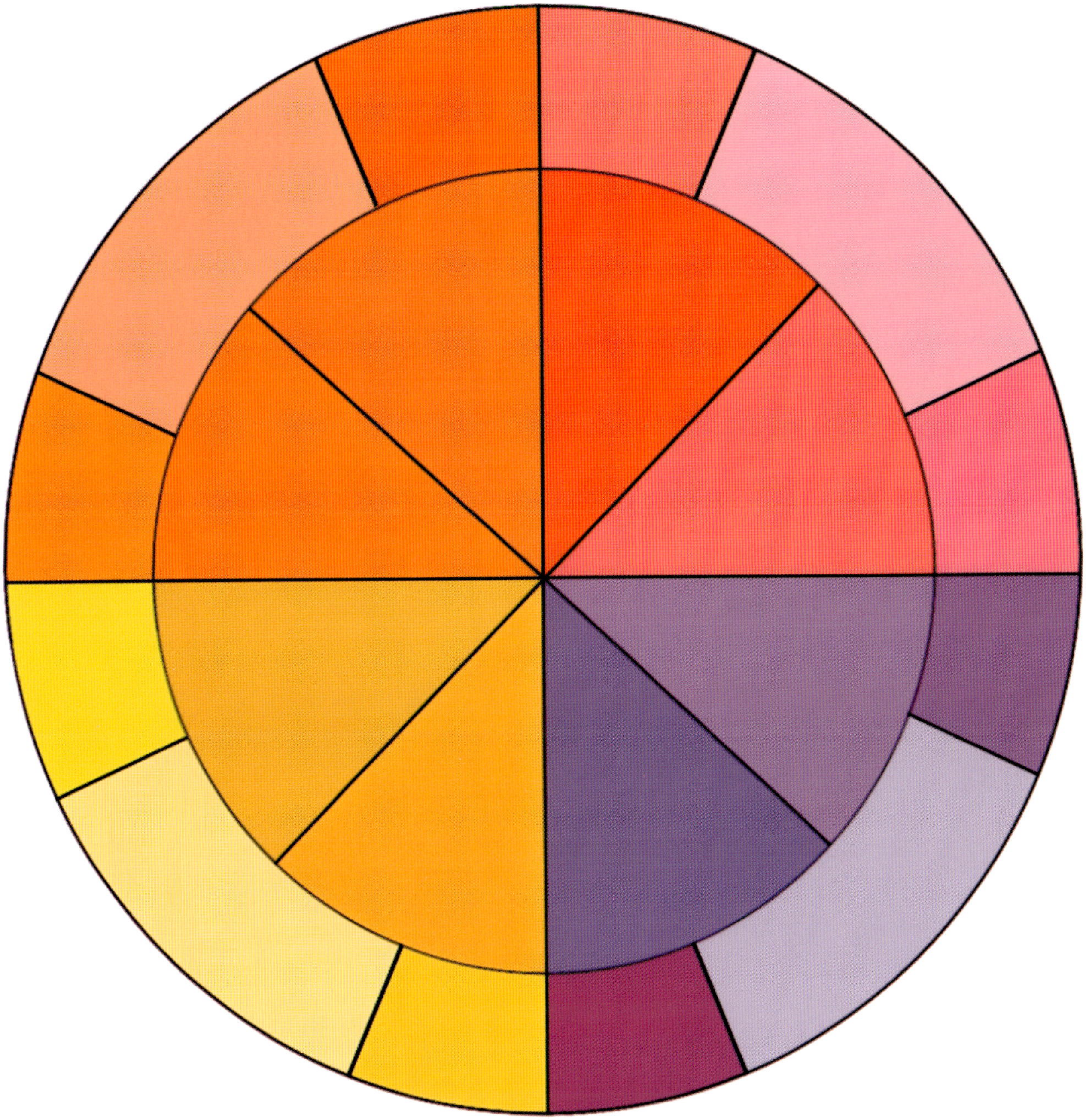

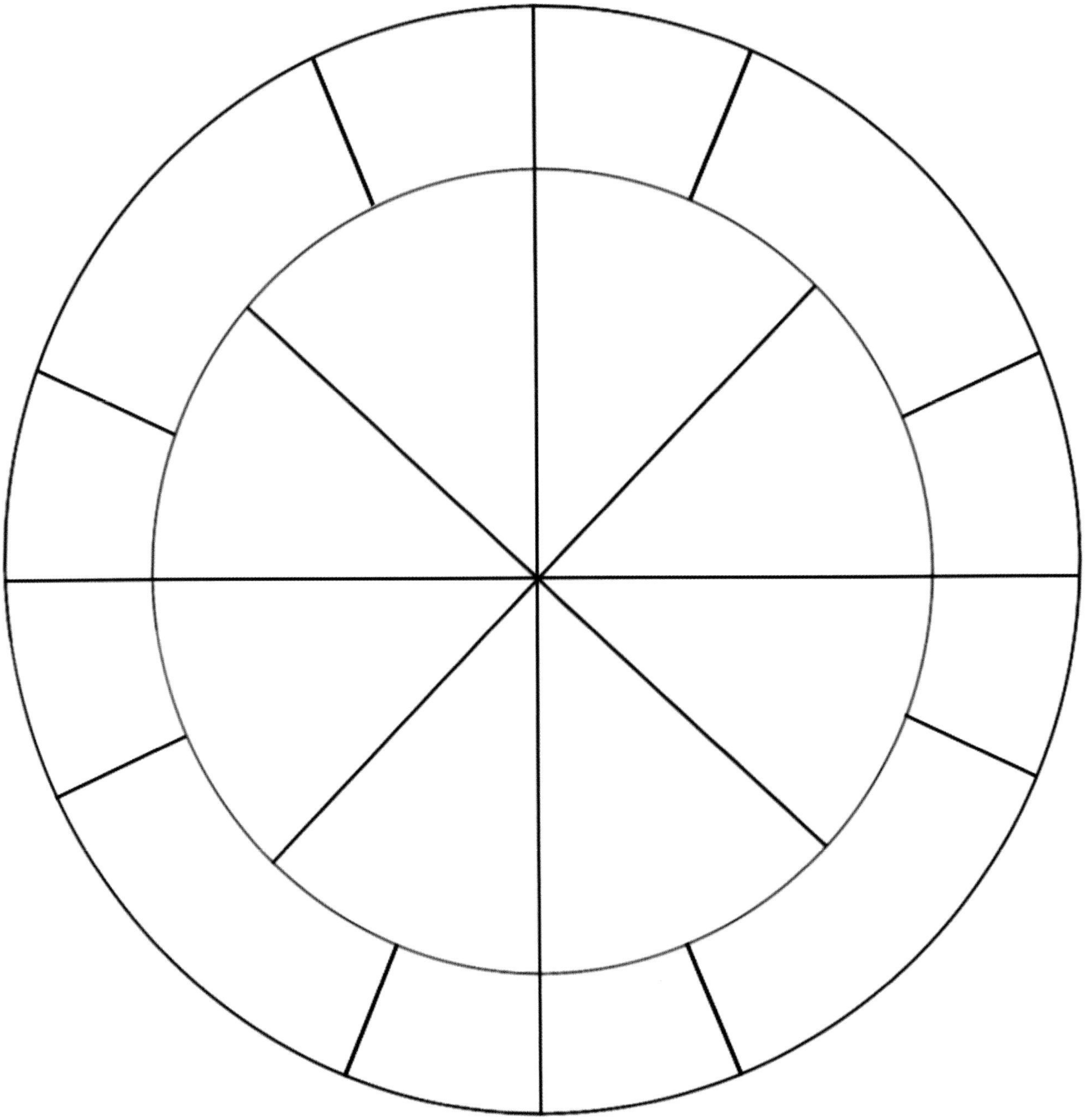

ACKNOWLEDGEMENTS

I finished writing this book two years to the day after the world shut down because of the COVID-19 pandemic. During that strange period of time, while physically isolated from many people, I learned firsthand how important it was to have an online collection of people with whom I enjoyed exchanging ideas and collaborating from afar.

Mark, El and Nova Robertson, who were photographer, stylist and assistant extraordinaires! It was amazing working with you and I'm just thrilled that you brought to life the photographs and ideas that were floating around in my head! I will never look at Victorian wallpaper or marble busts again without thinking about the house in Jim Thorpe!

Marisa and Liz, both of whom I met because of teaching workshops at Pennington Quilt Works in New Jersey, quickly organized virtual embroidery classes and handwork clubs. Planning those classes with them was an excellent distraction and it was even more enjoyable teaching my first Zoom classes with both of them at the helm.

Melissa Averinos graciously offered to create several original fabric art panels for me to use throughout the projects in my book. Collaborating with her was amazing and her support was invaluable!

Carmi, Danielle and Millie from John Bead are just the sweetest bunch of ladies that I have met in the crafting world. Chatting with them and planning beading projects was also a highlight during this time.

Daryl from Andover Fabrics, has been a constant source of encouragement and provided several of the fabrics that I used throughout this book.

Michele Muska, who I met years ago at a workshop at A Wing and a Prayer Farm in Vermont (also my favorite farm Instagram account!) has always been supportive anytime I have needed to ask a question or bounce ideas off of her!

And finally, working with Bruce and the entire team at Lucky Spool is always a positive experience. Being able to create a book from start to finish that is exactly what I pictured is amazing. I feel like, together, we created a book that would make Susanne proud!

Thank you all so much for your collaborative help!

Dedication

I feel like Leslie Knope always says it best :

"So find your team. Get to work. Whatever that work is that you find worth doing. Do it, and find some people to love who'll do it with you."

To Brett, Leo and Remy, you beautiful tropical fish, thank you for being on my team! I love you and I like you.

And to my parents for their love and support. I'm pretty sure they are the first ones to pre-order my book every single time!